Coastal crafts

Coastal crafts

DECORATIVE SEASIDE PROJECTS
to inspire your **inner beachcomber**

LARK
New York

LARK
New York

An Imprint of Sterling Publishing
1166 Avenue of the Americas
New York, NY 10036

ISBN 978-1-4547-0884-1

Distributed in Canada by Sterling Publishing
c/o Canadian Manda Group, 664 Annette
Street, Toronto, Ontario, Canada M6S 2C8
Distributed in the United Kingdom
by GMC Distribution Services
Castle Place, 166 High Street, Lewes,
East Sussex, England BN7 1XU
Distributed in Australia by Capricorn Link
(Australia) Pty. Ltd.
P.O. Box 704, Windsor, NSW 2756, Australia

For information about custom editions,
special sales, and premium and corporate
purchases, please contact Sterling
Special Sales at 800-805-5489 or
specialsales@sterlingpublishing.com.

Cover design by Jo Obarowski
Interior design by Karla Baker

Cover images: Starfish: Thinkstock: Wood:
Shutterstock. All other images: Cyhthia Shaffer

Interior images: Wood, Sand: Shutterstock;
all other images by Cynthia Shaffer

Manufactured in China

2 4 6 8 10 9 7 5 3 1

contents

INTRODUCTION   6

BASICS   8

Anchor & Sailboat Garland
and Gift Toppers   19

Sailboat-Embroidered Dish Towels   25

Charted Waters Lampshade   29

Coral Vases   33

Driftwood and Drill Sailboats   37

Driftwood-Framed Starfish   47

Gauze Bowls   53

Hanging Sea Glass   57

Sand and Shells Jars   61

It's A Shore Thing   67

Knotted Coaster Set   75

Message in a Bottle Necklace   81

Nautical Flags   87

Driftwood Seaside Village   91

Sand Memorabilia   95

River Rock Clock   99

Sand Letters   103

Sand and Jute Candlesticks   107

Heart Wreath   111

Starfish Greeting Cards   115

Linen Seashell Pillows   121

Stick Pencils   129

Stitched Fish Garland   133

TEMPLATES   136-142

ABOUT THE AUTHOR   143

ACKNOWLEDGMENTS   143

INDEX   144

introduction

I LOVE everything about the beach. I love the smell of the beach, the warmth of the sun and sand. I love to collect shells, and I love the sound of waves crashing on the shore. I love to boogie board with my boys! When I was a kid growing up in Southern California, vacations for my family always involved the beach. Sometimes we would rent a house right on the boardwalk in Newport Beach and sometimes we would camp at San Clemente State Beach. In fact, I was born in a hospital right there in Newport Beach, and my parents' first apartment together was on Balboa Island. My mom would always say that camping at the beach or renting a beach house provided the cheapest, most relaxing and entertaining time for everyone. And now, having a family of my own and going to the beach as much as possible, I could not agree with her more!

Over the years, my kids and I have been collecting seashells. Since much of our summertimes have been spent at the beach, we would of course go shelling . . . combing the beach for ocean treasures. I remember as a kid myself, lying on a beach towel on

my belly, sifting through the sand that was right there under my eyes . . . the sand was warm and felt so good passing through my fingers. And lying there . . . looking so closely at the sand, I would find some of the tiniest of shells and would stow them away in a little box I had with me. Of all the things I have taught my kids, the one that thrills me the most is their appreciation of the little tiny treasures we can find in nature if we take the time and just look. Yup, take the time and look.

Having so many glass jars full of seashells that were collected over the years, it seems appropriate that I should use these first in my beach and coastal crafts. As I was pawing through them, so many were just a part or pieces of a shell, which, at the time, seemed like such treasures.

Whether you're decorating all-out with coastal-themed rooms or just want a little snippet of a beach craft to remember a beach vacation, I'm sure you'll find plenty of projects and inspiration here to fill your needs.

Want that beach feeling all of your own? For starters, the color palette is always cool, refreshing, relaxing, and easy on the eyes. From sea-foam green, light aqua, and light tan to dusty reds and washed-up navy blues . . . add a little driftwood village to a sunroom, hang a nautical flag banner over a child's bed, fasten a distressed painted sign on the back fence or a pebble clock in an office.

Feel the beach and the coast by inviting the outside in!

Starting with the Basics section, you will find detailed information on how to make each project. For each project, there are step-by-step written instructions as well as step-by-step photographs to guide you along. For those projects that need templates, they are provided in a section at the back of the book, all clearly labeled.

I really want everyone, regardless of where you live, to be able to make these coastal crafts, so I tried to use materials that can be either found at the beach or purchased at your local craft store. While it's fun to craft with one-of-a-kind items, I really wanted this to be a "can do" kind of book! 'Cause after all, everyone deserves a little bit of beachy in their home, right?

So dive into *Coastal Crafts*. Swim through the pages and get hooked on crafting with sand, shells, burlap, and weathered wood, and add a little bit of beach to your life every day. After all, It's a Shore Thing that Life is a Beach!

Basics

Many of the materials you will find with these projects you might have lying around the house already, such as old sticks or seashells and sand collected in jars. In this section I will teach how to make those materials that you might not readily have. This Basics section is exactly what you need to create materials needed to make some of the projects, as well as turn your collected or found treasures into usable materials necessary to create your very own coastal crafts. Most of the materials and supplies you will need to make your coastal crafts can be found at your local craft store.

So if your collected treasures include seashells from your recent vacation, this is the place where you will find out exactly how to clean and preserve the shell back to its natural beauty. Or if you are looking to transform a pile of old sticks into beautiful driftwood to make a simple frame for a favorite starfish, you'll also find that tutorial right here.

Cleaning Seashells

There are several ways to clean seashells. Once you have decided which seashells you want to clean, take a minute and read over the following tutorials to determine which one will yield the best result for your shell. In some cases, a combination of cleaning methods is necessary.

Cleaning Seashells with Bleach

If your collection of shells has algae on them, or periostracum, a black leathery film covering them, then the following tutorial will help out.

WHAT YOU DO

1 Combine the 1 cup (250 mL) of bleach with the 1 cup (250 mL) of water in the small glass bowl (photo 1).

2 Carefully drop the seashells into the solution (photo 2).

3 Let the shells soak for at least 24 hours.

4 Check the shells and see if the algae or periostracum has come off and if the barnacles have softened up. Sometimes, they can be picked off at this stage.

5 If you are satisfied with the way the seashells look, then lift the shells out of the solution using the plastic spoon and rinse them thoroughly in the second cup of water.

6 Use the toothbrush to scrub the shells to get rid of any stubborn black algae or to release some of the barnacles (photo 3). A small chisel may be needed to lift off some really stuck barnacles (photo 4).

7 Place the cleaned seashells on a paper towel to drain and dry.

8 Once the seashells are dry, dip a clean paper towel into mineral oil and wipe onto the shells. The mineral oil brings out the colors and highlights the vibrancy of the shells (photo 5).

Cleaning Seashells with Hydrochloric Acid or Muriatic Acid

If your seashells have a white chalky film on them, this cleaning method will help to remove it and will bring out the natural colors and beauty.

GATHER

Seashells

2 small plastic containers

Large enough plastic container to place the smaller containers in

Plastic or latex gloves

Cup measure

3 cups (750 mL) water

½ cup (125 mL) hydrochloric acid or muriatic acid

Plastic fork

Paper towel

Mineral oil

WHAT YOU DO

1   Place one of the small containers in the large container.

2   While wearing the gloves, pour the hydrochloric or muriatic acid into the small container. Now add 1½ cups (375 mL) of water to the small container. Add 1½ cups (375 mL) of water to the second small container and place it in the larger container. Note: Since hydrochloric or muriatic acid is so caustic, the double containers help to keep it from touching any other surface (photo 1).

3   Slide one shell onto the prongs of the fork and then slowly lower the fork into the hydrochloric acid mixture. Keep the seashell in the mixture for approximately 4 seconds, then immediately dip it into the container of water. The seashell will bubble and fizz when in the hydrochloric solution (photo 2).

4   After the shells are dry, pop them into the hydrochloric or muriatic acid solution again and see if there is any remnant chalky film that needs to be removed, then immediately drop them into the water container.

5   Dip a clean paper towel into mineral oil and wipe it onto the shells. The mineral oil brings out the colors and highlights the vibrancy of the shells (photo 3).

Bleaching and Preserving Sand Dollars

To find a sand dollar intact is truly a treasure, but often they are discolored and fragile. This tutorial will help to brighten up the sand dollar and help to preserve and strengthen it, so that you can use it in your coastal craft project (photo 1).

1

GATHER

Sand dollars

2 small plastic containers

½ cup (125mL) bleach

½ cup (125 mL) water

Plastic fork

Soft toothbrush

Paper towels

White glue

1-inch (2.5 cm) foam brush

WHAT YOU DO

1. Combine the bleach and the water in one of the small plastic containers and then carefully drop the sand dollars into the solution. The sand dollars will float at first, so you may need to poke them down with the fork a bit to get them to lie flat on the bottom of the container (photo 2).

2. Allow the sand dollars to soak for about 10 minutes. When the 10 minutes are up, check them to see if you are satisfied with the whiteness. You may want to lightly brush the surface of the sand dollars with the toothbrush to loosen up any extra dirt. If you want the sand dollars even whiter, then soak them again for another 10 minutes.

   Note: *Do not leave the sand dollars in the solution overnight— they could dissolve!*

3. Lift the sand dollars out of the bleach and water solution and rinse at the sink with cool water (photo 3).

4. Pat the sand dollars with paper towels and allow them to completely dry before moving on to the next step.

5. Combine about a quarter-size drop of white glue with about the same amount of water.

6. Brush the glue mixture into the front and the back of each bleached sand dollar with the foam brush. Wait a few minutes and repeat (photo 4).

Making Driftwood

I'm fortunate enough to live pretty close to the beach, but since that's not the case for so many crafters, I thought that a tutorial on how to make your own driftwood would be a necessary thing for this book. Oh, sure, there are plenty of online sources to purchase driftwood, but, heck, why not just make your own and leave the beautiful driftwood along the shores to preserve nature's beauty? Driftwood can be found at almost every outdoor water source, such as rivers, oceans, and even freshwater lakes.

What type of wood works best? Oak and mahogany will be darker in color, but soft woods like pine, poplar, and birch will weather with a lighter finish or color. (If you can stick your thumbnail into the wood and make a mark, it is soft wood.) Since the wood I found was just out by a riverbed, I really don't know exactly what type of wood I'm using here.

WHAT YOU NEED TO GATHER

Sticks in a variety of widths and lengths, the drier the better

Chisel

Washing soda, or soda ash (sodium carbonate); Arm & Hammer makes a product called Super Washing Soda which would work

Hot water

Plastic container (with a lid) large enough to hold your wood sticks

Wire brush

Goggles

Rubber gloves

Towel

Small plastic container

Sandpaper in a couple of grits (100 and 180)

1-inch (2.5cm) foam brush

White paint

WHAT YOU DO

1   Gather the sticks together and place them on a hard surface, like a driveway or an old wood table. Depending on the project you have in mind, you may need to break some sticks down into shorter lengths (photo 1).

2   Working on one stick at a time, chisel off any dried bark that's peeling away (photo 2).

3   Fill the large plastic container with hot water from the tap. Add 4 cups (1 L) of washing soda to 2 gallons (8 L) of hot water, stirring continually until all the washing soda is dissolved (photo 3).

4   Carefully drop the sticks into the water and washing soda solution (photo 4).

5   You may need to place a heavy item like a rock over the sticks to keep them submerged; dry sticks tend to float (photo 5).

6   Soak the sticks in this solution with the lid on for 24 hours.

7   Check on the sticks a few times during the soaking period. You may want to use the wire brush and the chisel to scrub off any bark that has loosened during the soaking. Please wear gloves and the goggles to protect yourself!

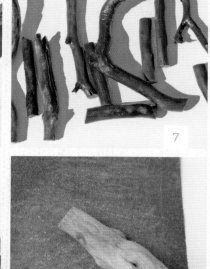

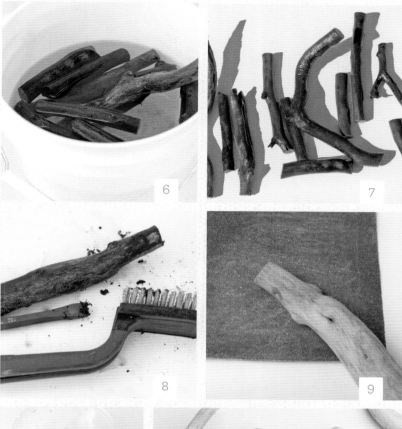

8. After the 24-hour period is over, take the sticks out of the solution and rinse them off thoroughly in cool water (photo 6).

9. Place the sticks on a towel out in the sun and let the sun dry them completely (photo 7).

10. Once the sticks are dry, use the chisel to remove any larger pieces of bark that might still be attached. Next, use sandpaper to round out the ends and to smooth any knots or branch stubs that might be sticking out. Start sanding with the 100-grit sandpaper and then finish with the 180 (photos 8–9).

11. In the small plastic container, mix up a small amount of white paint and water so that it looks a bit like cream (photo 10).

12. Paint the sticks with this solution, using the foam brush, and then wipe off the excess immediately. This will lighten and whiten up the sticks just a little bit more (photo 11).

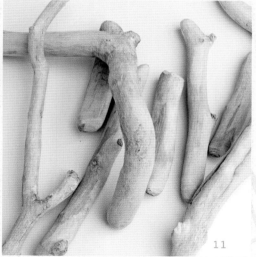

Anchor & Sailboat

GARLAND AND GIFT TOPPERS

Whether you make it your own or do exactly as you see here, salt dough crafts have been around for a long time—partly because once the dough dries it is virtually impossible to break or crack. This sailboat and anchor garland gives a new twist to this favorite craft that can be enjoyed by all ages, and for ages!

Ink pads in red and navy blue

Plastic drinking straw

Rubber stamp alphabet, ¼ inch (6 mm)

Cookie cooling rack

Fine sandpaper, 180 grit

3 yards (2.7 mm) of twine

Gold glitter

10 inches (25 cm) of gold ribbon

What You Do

1   Trace the Anchor Template A onto the copy paper with a fine-tip black marker. Turn the paper over to the back, and with the side of the soft lead pencil, sketch back and forth over the traced anchor image (photos 1–2).

2   Place the back side of the anchor onto the fun foam and trace around the image with a regular pencil, pressing lightly to avoid tearing the paper (photo 3).

3   Lift the paper off the fun foam to check that the entire image transferred (photo 3).

4   Use a craft knife and self-healing craft mat and cut out around the anchor (photo 4).

1

2

3

4

5

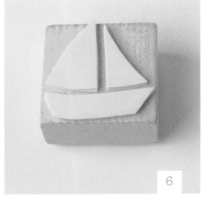

6

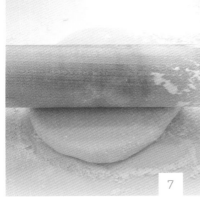

7

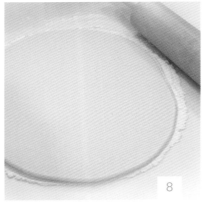

8

9

5   Glue the anchor to the wooden block and set aside to dry (photo 5).

6   Repeat steps 1–5 for Sailboat Template B, the sailboat motif. Glue the sailboat to the opposite side of the anchor block (photo 6).

7   Line a cookie sheet with parchment paper.

8   Mix together the flour, salt, and water in a mixing bowl. The dough will be stiff, like sugar cookie dough. Knead and fold the dough for 5 minutes. If the dough gets too stiff and starts to crack, add just a small amount of water to your hand, then work it into the dough ball by kneading and folding.

9   Form a ball with the dough. Place a small amount of flour onto a hard, smooth surface. Using a rolling pin, flatten the dough until it's an even ¼-inch (6 mm) thick (photos 7–8).

10 Press the larger cookie cutter into the dough. Using a spatula, carefully transfer the salt dough circle to the parchment-covered cookie sheet (photo 9).

11 To add some color, ink the foam sailboat with red ink and then gently press it into the salt dough circle, centered. Carefully lift the sailboat stamp up off the dough (photos 10 and 11).

12 Use a drinking straw to punch out a little hole at the top of the salt dough circle (photo 12).

13 Repeat steps 10–12 and make two more sailboat salt dough circles.

14 Repeat steps 10–12 and make three anchor salt dough circles, this time stamping the image with blue ink.

Note: *If you run out of dough, simply gather up the scraps and form a ball of dough again and then roll it out with the rolling pin.*

15 Press the smaller cookie cutter into the salt dough three times. Again, if you have run out of dough, simply gather up the scraps and form a ball of dough and then roll it out with the rolling pin.

16 Transfer the small salt dough circles to the parchment-lined cookie sheet using the spatula.

17 Stamp words like "ahoy matey," "come sail away," or "anchors aweigh" into the salt dough circles with the alphabet stamps and navy blue ink (photo 13).

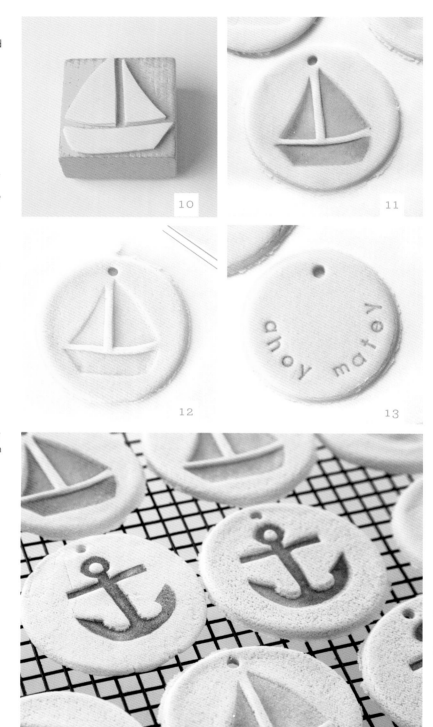

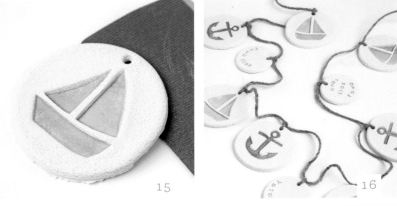

15

16

18 Use a drinking straw to punch out a little hole at the top of the salt dough circles.

19 Allow the salt dough circles to dry for 3 or 4 hours, and then carefully transfer them to the cookie cooling rack (photo 14).

20 Do not move the salt dough circles for several days! Depending on the moisture in the air, the drying time will vary. When they are no longer cool to the touch, then they are completely dry and super durable.

21 Use sandpaper to lightly clean up the outer edges and make them smooth (photo 15).

22 String the salt dough circles onto the twine. Alternate the anchors with the sailboats and add a word circle every now and then (photo 16).

23 As an option, add gold glitter to the dough and knead and fold it in until the glitter is evenly distributed. Punch out a circle with the large cookie cutter and then stamp the circle with the sailboat and red ink. After the circle is completely dry, tie onto a gold ribbon and use as a gift topper.

Sailboat-embroidered

DISH TOWELS

Quick-and-easy embroidered dish towels make the perfect hostess gift for the person who loves all things coastal and nautical.

WHAT YOU NEED TO GATHER

Sailboat Template 1 (page 137)

Sailboat Template 2 (page 137)

Sailboat Template 3 (page 137)

Sailboat Template 4 (page 137)

3 white flour sack dish towels, 28 x 28 inches (71 x 71 cm)

Water-soluble marking pen

Ruler

6-inch (15 cm) embroidery hoop

Perle cotton or embroidery floss in the following colors: light blue, light aqua, teal, peach, dusty coral, and rose

Embroidery needle or a sharp needle with a large enough eye to thread the perle cotton or embroidery floss

Paper towel

What You Do

THREE GREEN SAILBOATS

1   Fold the dish towel in half and press along the fold to make a center line. You can form this crease by pressing the fold with an iron or by simple running the back of your fingernail along the fold (photo 1).

2   Make several marks with the water-soluble pen, 2½ inches (6.4 cm) up from the hem

3   Place the dish towel on top of Sailboat Template 1, centered on the crease and with the sailboat sitting right on the mark that is 2½ inches (6.4 cm) up from the hem. Trace the motif with the water-soluble pen (photo 2). Shift the dish towel over slightly to the left and trace Sailboat Template 2, again with the sailboat sitting right on the mark that is 2½ inches (6.4 cm) up from the hem. Shift the dish towel over to the right of the center sailboat, and trace Sailboat Template 3. Make sure that the bottoms of all three sailboats sit right at that indicated mark, 2½ inches (6.4 cm) up from the bottom (photo 3).

4   Fasten the dish towel into the embroidery hoop (photo 4).

5   Using double thread and a needle, backstitch around the sailboat motifs (photo 5).

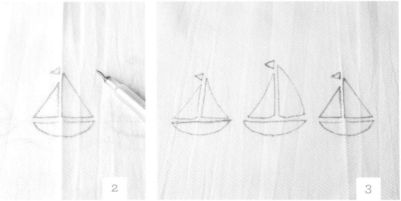

5

6 Dampen a paper towel with water and daub the dish towel and the embroidery until the water-soluble pen marks disappear.

THREE CORAL SAILBOATS

1 Repeat steps 1 and 2 from the above instructions.

2 Place the dish towel on top of Sailboat Template 2, centered on the crease. Trace the motif with the water-soluble pen. Shift the dish towel over slightly to the left and trace Sailboat Template 1. Shift the dish towel over to the right of the center sailboat, and trace Sailboat Template 3. Make sure that the bottoms of the boats sit right at that indicated mark, 2½ inches (6.4 cm) up from the bottom.

3 Repeat steps 4–6 (Three Green Sailboats) to finish this dish towel.

ONE BIG SAILBOAT

1 Repeat steps 1 and 2 from the Three Green Sailboats instructions.

2 Place the dish towel on top of Sailboat Template 4, centered on the crease. Trace the motif with the water-soluble pen. Make sure that the bottom of the wave sits right at that indicated mark, 2½ inches (6.4 cm) up from the bottom.

3 Repeat steps 4–6 (Three Green Sailboats) to finish this dish towel.

Charted
waters
LAMPSHADE

This quick, no-fuss charted lampshade project will brighten up any room and give it just a bit of coastal charm.

2 large pages from a nautical chart kit, 22 x 17½ inches (56 x 44 cm)

1 white cloth lampshade: 9-inch (23-cm) diameter at the bottom, 7-inch (18-cm) diameter at the top, 8 inches (20 cm) high

Liquitex Matte Gel

Old paintbrush

Scissors

Sisal rope: 44 lb (20 kg), ¼ inch (6 mm), 3½ yards (3.2 m)

Hot glue gun and hot glue

White chalk

What You Do

1   Tear or cut a section out of the chart kit pages that looks interesting or has fun and bright colors that you like. This piece can be any size, but the bigger the panel, the quicker the lampshade will be covered with the paper (photo 1).

2   Place the cut or torn page piece on the lampshade, snug up against the top edge but just under the very top binding. You may need to trim the top edge of the page piece into a slight concave curve to better fit around the lampshade (photo 2).

3   Use the paintbrush to apply Matte Gel to the lampshade where the paper panel will be adhered. Place the paper panel against the lampshade on top of the gel and then apply a coat to the top of the paper. Brush the Matte Gel on evenly to avoid any streaks.

> **tip**
>
> Start from the center of the panel and move out to the sides to avoid the formation of air bubbles.

4   Continue to add Matte Gel and page pieces to the lampshade, overlapping them so the fabric on the lampshade is completely covered. You can cut these page pieces, or, if you want a more haphazard look, tear the chart kit pages. As the page pieces start to reach the bottom of the lampshade, you

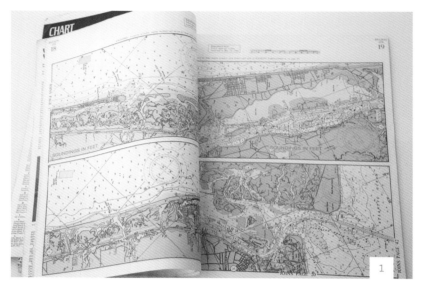

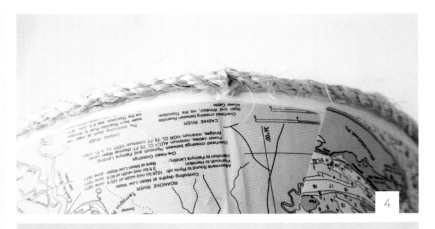

4

5

may need to trim into a slight convex curve to fit snug against the bottom edge.

5   Cut or tear out interesting portions of the chart kit pages that you want to highlight, such as the compass or large words that make a statement. Adhere them on top of the lampshade so that they stand out (photo 3).

6   Set the lampshade aside to dry.

7   Wrap the sisal rope around the top of the lampshade, over the binding. Mark the sisal so that the beginning and the end butt together. Cut two lengths of sisal for the top (photo 4).

8   Repeat step 7 for the bottom edge of the lampshade.

9   Glue one length of sisal rope to the very top edge of the lampshade with hot glue. Start by placing a small amount of hot glue to the back of the lampshade and attaching just the beginning end of the sisal. Add hot glue to small portions of the lampshade as you work your way around until you reach the beginning. Make sure that the ends of the sisal are butted up snug together. If there is a little bit of overlap, trim the excess off.

10   Repeat step 9 for the second length of sisal rope, placing it just under the first rope. With this second sisal rope in place, the entire bound edge should be completely covered (photo 5).

11   Repeat steps 9 and 10 for the lower edge of the lampshade.

Coral
VASES

No painting experience is needed to transform plain white vases into handpainted treasures. Using a series of dots, follow the stencil and within minutes you'll be ready to add a flower arrangement to freshen up a bathroom or kitchen table.

WHAT YOU NEED TO GATHER

Coral Template A (page 138)

Coral Template B (page 138)

Coral Template C (page 138)

3 white vases in varying sizes (large: 4 x 4 x 8¼ inches [10 x 10 x 21 cm]; medium: 2¾ x 2¾ x 4 ¾ inches [7 x 7 x 12 cm]; small: 3 x 3 x 3¾ inches [7.7 x 7.7 x 9.5 cm])

3 sheets of copy paper

Soft lead pencil (9B)

Regular pencil (2B)

Black fine-tip marker

Rubbing alcohol

Paper towels

Scissors

Masking tape

Multisurface satin paint in poppy and pumpkin (Americana brand)

2 small disposable containers

Paintbrushes in 2 different sizes, one medium and one small

What You Do

1. Lay the large vase down on its side, onto a sheet of copy paper, and trace around the perimeter of the vase (photo 1).

2. Lay the traced image onto Coral Template A for the large vase, B for the medium vase, or C for the small vase, and then trace the coral shape within the traced vase image using the black fine-tip marker. Note: You may need to adjust the shape of the coral motif to fill the space of your vase. Extend the branches, add, or delete branches to your liking (photo 2).

3. Daub rubbing alcohol onto the paper towel and then wipe the surface of the vase to get rid of any oil from your hands that might be on the vase (photo 3).

4. Cut out the vase shape and then flip it over to the back. Use the soft lead pencil and trace back over the coral motif, using the side of the pencil to create a thick, sketchy mark (photo 4).

5. Flip the vase template over so it's right side up and then use masking tape to adhere it to the vase (photo 6).

6. Using the regular pencil, trace back over the coral motif. Press down hard with the pencil to make sure that the image is transferring onto the vase. Remove the masking tape and check to make sure that all the marks have transferred (photo 7).

7. Place a small amount of the poppy-colored paint in a disposable container.

8   Using the medium-size paintbrush, dip the rounded end into the paint and dot it straight up and down onto the vase, right over the pencil mark. Repeat this until you have dots along every traced pencil mark (photos 8–10).

Note: Make smaller dots as you reach the ends of the coral by dotting once with a fully loaded paintbrush end and then making the next dot with the paint left on the end of the paintbrush. In other words, do not dip the end of the paintbrush in the paint for each and every dot you make.

9   Place a small amount of the pumpkin-colored paint into the other disposable container.

10   Using the small paintbrush, dip the rounded end into the paint and dot it straight up and down onto the vase, but on the left side of the painted dots that are already on the vase. Repeat this until you have dots along every coral branch (photo 11).

11   Set the vase aside to dry. Per the manufacturer's specifications, curing of the paint can take up to seven days.

12   Once the paint has cured, wipe off the pencil marks (photo 12).

Note: For the other two vases, repeat the above steps using Coral Templates B and C, and use only the small paintbrush to dot the paint onto the vases, skipping step 10. The smaller vases have only one line of poppy-colored dots to create the coral motif.

Driftwood
and drill
SAILBOATS

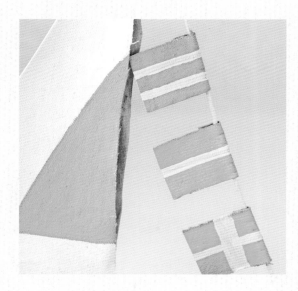

These easy-to-make driftwood sailboats make the perfect place setting at your next outdoor dinner.

WHAT YOU NEED
TO GATHER

Driftwood Sailboat
Template A (page 139)

Driftwood Sailboat
Template B (page 139)

Driftwood Sailboat
Template C (page 139)

Driftwood Sailboat
Template D (page 139)

9 pieces of driftwood, 5 to 6
inches (13–15 cm) long

6 wood craft sticks, 4½ x ⅝
inches (11 x 1.5 cm)

Ruler

Pencil

Electric drill and drill bits

Wood glue

24⅜ inch (10mm) No. 3 tacks

Small hammer

¼ yard (23 cm) natural color
drill fabric

Acrylic paint: white, sea-foam
green, aqua, yellow, and
dusty red

Kitchen scissors

Paintbrush

⅛-inch (3mm) hole-punch

Large-eye needle

White cotton string,
5 yards (4.5 m)

3 sticks, 8 inches (20 cm)
long and ¼ inch (6 mm)
in diameter

White glue

6 paper clips

3 coins: 1 quarter, 1 nickel,
1 penny

What You Do

AQUA STRIPE AND PENNANT SAILBOAT

1   Place three pieces of driftwood of roughly the same length next to one another.

2   Cut down two wood craft sticks to measure 2¼ inches (5.7 cm) each.

3   Place the cut craft sticks across the driftwood and mark with a pencil where the tacks will be placed, one at each piece of driftwood, for each craft stick (photo 1).

4   Drill a hole slightly larger than the tack at each mark. Put a small drop of wood glue on top of each drilled hole (photo 2).

5   Place the wood craft sticks on the driftwood again and hammer the tacks into place. Set aside for the glue to dry. Repeat for the other side (photo 3).

6   Flip the driftwood structure over and mark with a pencil the center of the middle piece of driftwood.

7   Drill a hole at this mark that is slightly bigger than one of the 8-inch (20 cm) sticks, which will be used as the mast (photo 4).

8   Fill the drilled hole with wood glue and then push the "mast" stick into the hole (photo 5). Adjust the stick slightly to make sure that it is standing up as straight as possible. Set aside to dry (photo 6).

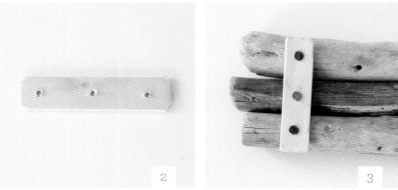

9 Hammer a tack at both ends of the middle piece of driftwood (photo 7).

10 Cut out one of Driftwood Sailboat Template A and three of Driftwood Sailboat Template D from the drill fabric.

11 Paint the sail white (photo 8). Paint two pennants sea-foam green and one pennant yellow (photo 9).

12 Once the sail is dry, mark horizontal lines as follows: 1⅛ inches up from the bottom, 2¼ inches (5.7 cm) up from the bottom, 3¾ inches (8.3 cm) up from the bottom, and 4¼ (10.8 cm) inches up from the bottom (photo 10). Paint the marked stripes aqua (photos 11–12).

13 Punch holes in the corners of the sail (photo 13).

14 Thread a large-eye needle with cotton string. Thread the string through the punched holes in the sail (photo 14), and then wrap the string around the mast stick, at the bottom, about ½ inch (1.3 cm) up from the driftwood (photo 16). Then knot the string. Repeat for the top of the mast (photo 15) and the side of the sail, except attach the string to the tack.

15 Cut a length of string 14 inches (36 cm). Mark the center of the string with a pencil.

16 Glue the yellow pennant to the string center at the mark. Glue the other two pennants to the string, ½ inch (1.3 cm) from the yellow pennant, on either side. Place paper clips where the pennants fold over

the string to keep them in place while the glue dries (photo 17).

17 Once the glue is dry, tie and knot the pennant string to the top of the mast stick and then to the end tack.

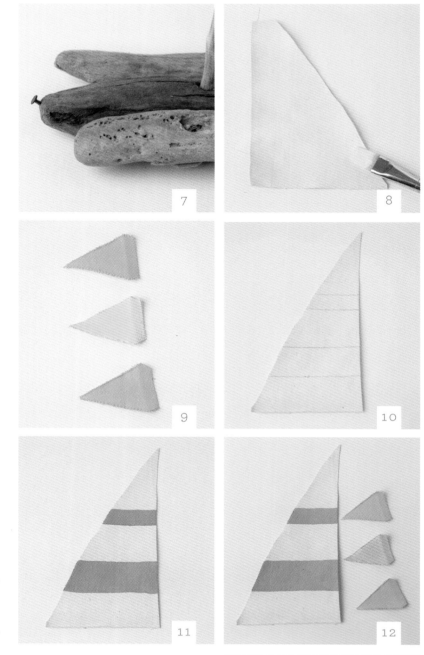

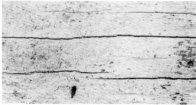

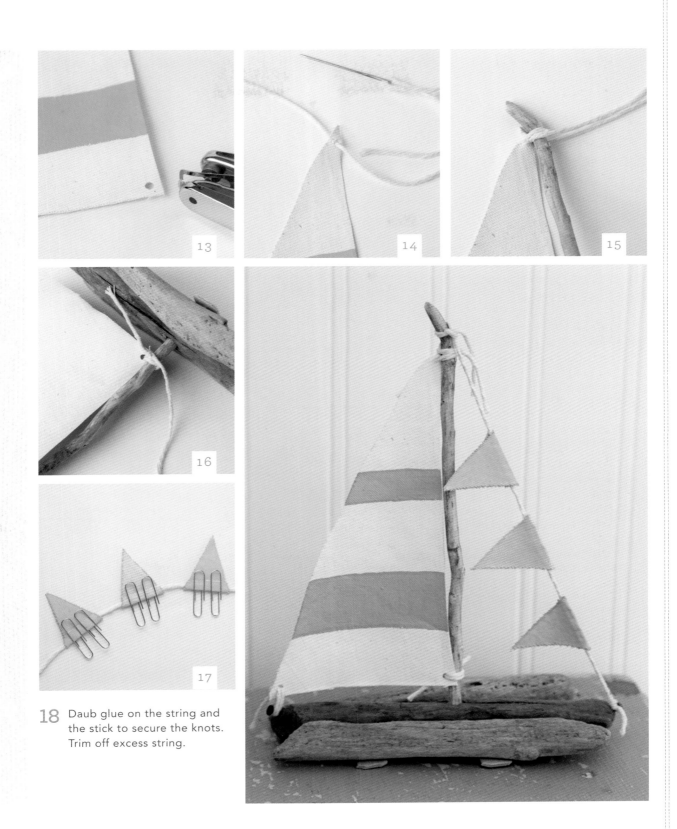

18 Daub glue on the string and the stick to secure the knots. Trim off excess string.

18

19

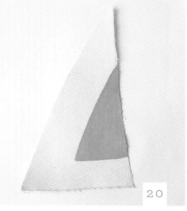

20

DUSTY RED AND FLAG SAILBOAT

1   Repeat steps 1–9 from the Aqua Stripe and Pennant Sailboat.

2   Cut out one of Driftwood Sailboat Template A and three of Driftwood Sailboat Template C from the drill fabric.

3   Paint the sail white. Paint one flag dusty red. Mix a drop of yellow paint with the red paint and then paint the second flag. Add a second drop of yellow to this mixture and paint the third flag (photo 18). Paint stripes on the flags with white paint (photo 19).

4   Draw a triangle on the sail and then paint inside the triangle with the dusty red paint (photo 20).

5   Punch holes in the corners of the sail.

6   Thread a large-eye needle with cotton string. Thread the string through the punched holes and then wrap around the mast stick, at the bottom, about ½ inch (1.3 cm) up from the driftwood (photo 21). Knot the string. Repeat for the top of the sail and the side, except attach that string to the end tack.

7   Cut a length of string 14 inches (36 cm). Mark the center of the string with a pencil.

8   Glue one flag to the string at the center mark. Glue the other two flags to the string, ½ inch (1.3 cm) from the center flag, on either side. Place paper clips where the flags fold over the string to keep them in place while the glue dries.

9   Once the glue is dry, tie and knot the flag string to the top of the mast stick and then to the end tack.

10 Daub glue on the string and the stick to secure the knots. Trim off excess string.

THREE CIRCLE SEA-FOAM GREEN SAILBOAT

1   Repeat steps 1–9 from the Aqua Stripe and Pennant Sailboat.

2   Cut out one of Driftwood Sailboat Template A and one of Driftwood Sailboat Template B from the drill fabric.

3   Paint the large sail white. Paint the small sail sea-foam green. Set aside to dry (photo 22).

4   Place the quarter, nickel, and penny on the white sail and trace around them with a pencil (photo 23).

5   Paint the circles with the sea-foam green paint (photo 24).

6   Punch holes in the corners of the sail.

7   Thread a large-eye needle with cotton string. Thread the string through the punched holes in the white sail with the green circles and then wrap the string around the mast stick, at the bottom, about ½ inch (1.3 cm) up from the driftwood. Repeat for the top of the mast and the side of the sail, except attach that string to the end tack.

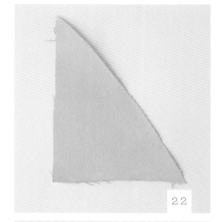

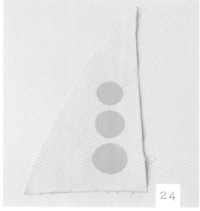

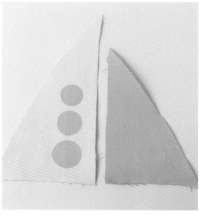

8   Thread the string through the punched holes in the sea-foam green sail and then wrap the string around the mast stick, at the bottom, about ½ inch (1.3 cm) up from the driftwood. Knot the string. Repeat for the top of the sail and the side, except attach that string to the end tack.

9   Daub glue on the string and the stick to secure the knots. Trim off the excess string.

nets
Wh les
STAR
Starfish
seaweed
Seahorse
star•fish (stär′fish′), n., pl. (esp. collectively) -fish, (esp. for kinds or species) -fish•es. any echinoderm of the class Asteroidea, having a radial body, usu. in the form of a star, with five or more arms radiating from a central disk. Also called sea star. [1530–40]

Driftwood -framed

STARFISH

Hang this driftwood frame from a windowsill or in a bathroom to bring a bit of sea life inside.

WHAT YOU NEED
TO GATHER

4 pieces of driftwood, 9 to 11 inches (23 x 28 cm) long

Craft wire (2 yards (12 m), 20 gauge) cut into 4 lengths, 18 inches (46 cm) each

Wire cutters

Needle-nose pliers

⅛ yard (12 cm) of natural colored muslin, torn into 4 strips of 1 x 30 inches (2.5 x 76 cm)

Hot glue and hot glue gun

White acrylic paint

White craft glue

Old paintbrush

1 sheet craft-colored paper

Ruler

1 transparency sheet

Double-sided tape

Black marker

4 small light blue eyelets

1 sheet white copy paper

1 piece light blue card stock, 3¼ x ⅝ inch (8 x 2 cm)

1 piece of black mat board, 3⅜ x ¾ inches (8.6 x 2 cm)

1 yard (91 cm) white cotton string

Starfish, 5 x 5 inches (13 x 13 cm)

24 inches (61 cm) of fishing line

What You Do

1   Arrange the four sticks into a box or frame (photo 1).

2   Secure one of the wires around the end of one of the pieces using the needle-nose pliers (photo 2).

3   Wrap the wire around a second piece of driftwood several times and secure in place (photo 3).

4   Repeat steps 2 and 3 for the remaining pieces of driftwood (photo 4).

    Note: *The frame may not feel very secure at this point. The wires are there to keep the driftwood from shifting as the strips of muslin are wrapped around the corners of the frame.*

5   Using hot glue, secure one end of a strip of muslin to the driftwood where the wire is holding the corners together (photo 5).

6   Wrap the muslin around the corner until the wire is completely covered. Secure the end of the muslin with a small amount of hot glue (photo 6).

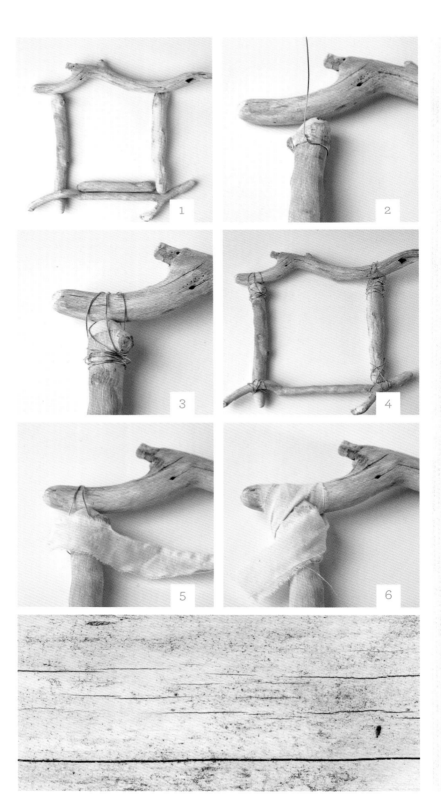

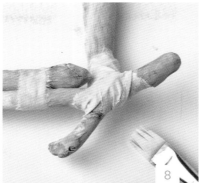

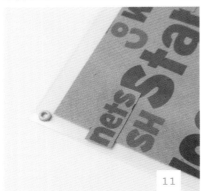

7   Repeat steps 5 and 6 for the remaining three corners (photo 7).

8   Combine 1 tablespoon (30 mL) of white glue with 1 tablespoon (15 mL) of water and ½ teaspoon (2.5 mL) of white acrylic paint.

9   Paint the muslin corners with the paint and glue mixture and then set the frame aside to dry completely (photo 8).

10 Gather some fun, seafaring words and cut them out and arrange on the craft paper. Once you have an arrangement you like, glue the words onto the paper.

11 Measure inside the frame. Cut the word scramble to be ¾ inch (1.9 cm) narrower and shorter then the frame dimensions.

Note: *The word scramble is larger than the frame, so there will be extra words left.*

12 With the remaining craft paper, cut out words that look interesting and glue them onto the larger word panel from step 11 (photo 9).

13 Measure the word panel from step 11 and then cut out two pieces from the transparency ½ inch (1.3 cm) wider and longer than the word panel.

14 Sandwich the word panel between the transparencies and secure in place with very small pieces of double-sided tape.

15 Mark a small dot in each corner with the black marker (photo 10).

16 Set an eyelet in each corner where the black mark is (photo 11).

17 Create a small starfish definition on a computer. Adjust the size so that when the definition is cut out it is slightly smaller than the piece of light blue card stock.

18 Layer the definition on top of the light blue card stock and then onto the black mat board, gluing them into place (photo 13).

19 Glue the definition panel onto the word panel.

20 Thread cotton string through the eyelets and then around the frame and secure with small knots. Repeat for the other three eyelets.

21 Wrap a length of white string around one of the arms of the starfish several times and then around the top of the frame and secure with a small knot (photo 14).

22 Apply a small dab of glue to all the knots. After the glue is dry, hang the driftwood-framed starfish with fishing line.

13

14

15

Gauze
BOWLS

These simple and elegant gauze bowls are perfect for decorating a coffee table filled with collected seashells, or for a guest bathroom filled with sea-salt bath bombs.

WHAT YOU NEED TO GATHER

Large plastic trashbag

Plastic wrap

1 medium-size mixing bowl

Masking tape or large rubber band

Disposable container

White glue

Water

Acrylic paint in cool water colors, Multi-Surface Satin (Americana brand)

Old spoon

3 yards (2.7 m) of gauze

Scissors

Large plastic cup

What You Do

1. Cover the work surface with the large plastic trashbag.

2. Cover the outside of the bowl with plastic wrap. To secure the plastic wrap, tape it to the inside of the bowl or secure it with a rubber band. Place the bowl upside down on the work surface (photo 1).

3. In a disposable container, mix together ½ cup (125 mL) of glue, 2 tablespoons (3 mL) of water, and about 1 teaspoon (5 mL) of the acrylic paint. The more paint you add to the mixture, the darker in color the bowl will be (photo 2).

4. Cut a piece of gauze and drape it over the plastic-wrapped bowl. Paint the gauze with the glue-water-paint mixture (photo 3).

5. Continue adding an additional layer of gauze, overlapping until the bowl is completely covered.

6. Lift the bowl up and off the work surface and place the large plastic cup under it.

7. Cover the gauzed bowl with a final layer of gauze and paint with the glue mixture. This time, allow the gauze to drape down the bowl, creating an interesting upper edge (photo 4).

8. Double check to make sure that all the gauze is saturated with the glue mixture.

9. Set the bowl aside to dry.

10. Once the glue has dried, lift the gauze bowl off the bowl and then peel off the plastic wrap.

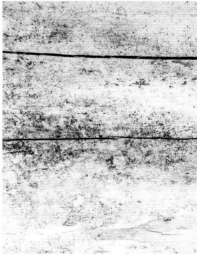

Hanging
SEA GLASS

Whether it's sea glass you have been collecting for years or sea glass you recently purchased, this easy project will add a touch of ocean color to a backyard patio or your favorite white cupboard door.

WHAT YOU NEED TO GATHER

Driftwood or old dried stick, 20 inches long and 3½ inches (51 x 8.9 cm) in circumference

Water

Sandpaper

Old rag

White paint

6 small plastic disposable mixing containers

Old paintbrush

Blue sea glass, 17 pieces in various sizes and shapes

Green sea glass, 12 pieces in various sizes and shapes

Purple sea glass, 6 pieces in various sizes, shapes, and intensity

Kitchen scissors

Clear or white sea glass, 1 piece

Craft paper

6-lb (2.7 kg) fishing line, 10 yards (9 m)

12-lb (5.5 kg) fishing line, 1 yard (1 m)

Clear or light yellow epoxy

6 wood stir sticks or popsicle sticks

What You Do

1. Sand the driftwood with the sandpaper and wipe it clean with an old rag.

2. If the color of the wood is to your liking, then move on to the next step. If you want to lighten the stick up a bit, dilute white paint with water in a disposable container. Combine 1 tablespoon (15 mL) of paint with 1 teaspoon (5 mL) of water and stir. Paint the stick with the diluted paint mixture and then quickly wipe the excess paint off with the old rag, working in small sections at a time. Continue until the entire stick has been painted and wiped off. Set the stick aside to dry.

3. Gather all the sea glass and arrange the pieces in six rows with six pieces in each row, one color per row, ordered as described in the following steps (photo 1).

4. Starting with the blue glass, arrange one row with the largest piece of glass at the top and with the glass pieces getting smaller and lighter in color as you get toward the end of the row.

5. The next row of glass should be green. Again, start with the largest piece of glass at the top, with the pieces getting smaller and lighter in color as you get toward the end of the row.

6. The third row of hanging sea glass is blue. Follow step 4, except replace the last blue piece of glass with a clear or white piece.

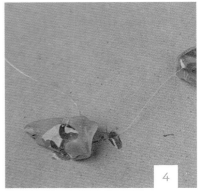

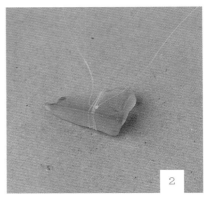

7. The fourth row is green. Repeat step 5.

8. The fifth row is made with the purple sea glass. Arrange this row with the largest piece of purple glass at the top and with the glass pieces getting smaller and lighter in color as you get toward the end of the row.

9. And, finally, the last row of hanging glass is made with more blue glass. Follow step 4.

10. Cut a length of 6-lb (2.7 kg) fishing line 1½ yards (1.4 m).

11. Starting with one end of the fishing line and the last piece of sea glass in each row, carefully wrap the fishing line around the sea glass several times. Look for divots in the glass that the fishing line can sink into or grab onto. Knot the fishing line several times (photo 2).

12. Pick up the next piece of sea glass in the row and wrap the fishing line around it, 3 inches (7.6 cm) from the first piece of tied glass (photo 3).

13 Repeat step 12 until all six pieces of sea glass in a row are tied onto the fishing line.

14 Lay the tied sea glass row on a piece of craft paper with the knots above.

15 Following the manufacturer's instructions, mix up a small amount of epoxy in a disposable container with a stir stick. Make sure there is good ventilation when you're working with the epoxy.

16 Once the mixing is complete, daub the epoxy on each piece of sea glass right where the fishing line knot is. For a secure hold, continue to daub epoxy on the fishing line and the sea glass. The epoxy will dry clear and not be noticeable (photo 4).

17 Repeat steps 14–16 for the remaining five rows of sea glass.

18 Let the epoxy dry or set for several hours before moving on to the next step.

19 Tie the first blue hanging sea glass strand to the driftwood stick about 5 inches (13 cm) from the end. Knot the fishing line several times. Trim off any excess fishing line (photos 3 and 5).

20 Repeat step 19 for each of the remaining five strands of hanging sea glass. Space the rows 2 inches (6 cm) apart.

21 Cut a length from the 12-lb (5.5 kg) fishing line measuring 1 yard (1 m). Tie the fishing line to each end of the drift- wood stick, 3 inches (7.6 cm) in.

Sand
and shells
JARS

These hanging wired jars will illuminate any backyard gathering with the right amount of twinkle needed for that special family gathering or celebration.

What You Do

1 Place the jar on the paper and trace around the base of the jar with the pencil (photo 1).

2 Use the wire for the 6½" bottom loop and curve it into the shape of the traced circle (photo 2). The wire circle will be slightly smaller than the traced circle.

3 Create a loop at one end of the wire using the round-nose pliers and then slip the opposite end into this loop, hooking the wires together to form the bottom loop (photo 2).

4 Using the round-nose pliers, turn up one end of a side wire to make a loop (photo 3). Hook this loop onto the bottom wire loop created in step 3 and then twist the end around a couple of times (photo 4).

5 Repeat step 4 for all five of the other side wires. Alternate the order of the wires so that the shorter wires are in between the longer wires (photo 5).

6 Using the round-nose pliers, create a loop in the wires 2½ inches (6.4 cm) up from where they are attached to the bottom loop (photo 6).

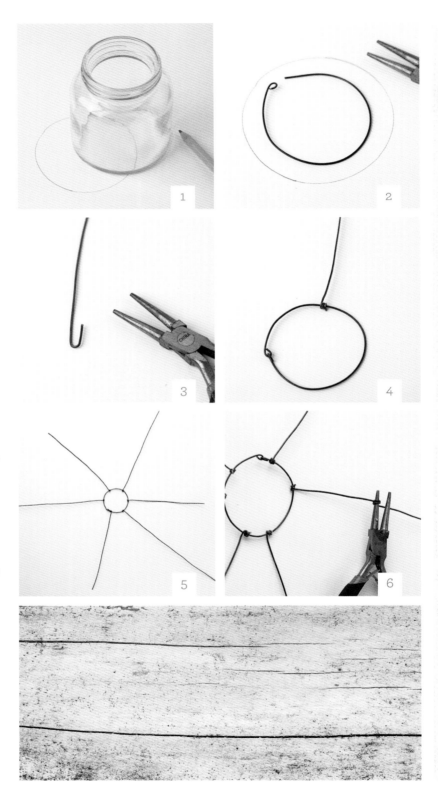

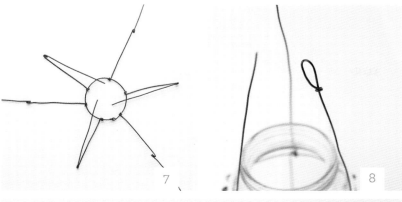

7   Fold the shorter wires back down toward the bottom wire loop and secure them around that bottom wire loop, using the round-nose pliers. Note: these shorter wires will form a triangle of sorts with a small loop or hole at the top of the triangle where the outer wire is threaded through (photo 7).

8   Place the wire base you have just created on top of the traced circle. Bend all the wires up at 45-degree angles where the wires each meet the traced circle.

9   Thread the side loop wire through the loops in all the side wires, then place the jar in the resulting wire hanger.

10 While the jar is in the hanger, create a loop at one end of the side wire using the round-nose pliers and then slip the opposite end of the wire into this loop and hook the wires together (photo 8).

11 Bend back 1 inch (2.5 cm) of the 12-inch (30 cm) wire and then form a secure loop.

12 Wrap the two remaining wires around the base of this loop (photo 9).

13 Carefully drill small holes in each of the nine seashells, using a Dremel tool and small drill bit.

14 Cut nine various lengths of steel wire.

15 Loop a wire through the hole in each shell and secure. Create a loop on the other end of the wire and hook around the bottom loop. Close this loop to secure the hanging wire to the seashell (photo 10).

16 Remove the jar from the wire hanger. Note: You may need to bend the top long wire a bit in order to release the jar.

17 Paint the bottom of the jar with white glue. Paint the glue on the sides in a wavy pattern (photo 11).

18 Push the jar into the sand and press and roll until all the glue is covered with sand (photo 12).

19 Stand the jar upside down to dry. Once dried, lightly rub the jar to release any extra sand (photo 13).

20 Fill the jar with about 1 inch (2.5 cm) of sand and then place the jar back into the wire hanger. Drop a small white candle or tea light into the jar and push it down into the sand a bit.

tip

1 Choose jars with openings large enough for a candle to fit inside.

2 Use driftwood or wire-wrapped sea glass in place of the seashells.

3 Use jars that are colored.

10

11

12

13

it's a Shore thing
WALL HANGING

Whether it's weathered wood or new wood that's been weathered, this scrappy lettered sign will be welcomed on any fence in the backyard or lake house.

Paintbrushes in a variety of sizes

Acrylic paint: mint green, teal, light blue, light aqua, dark aqua, blue, dark purple, and light purple

Disposable containers with lids

20 1¼-inch (3.2 cm) screws

Electric screwdriver

What You Do

1   Lightly sand the edges and all the surfaces of all the boards (photos 1–2).

2   Dampen an old rag and clean the dust and dirt off the boards.

3   Paint the fronts with the white house paint. Paint all the boards to the very edge, except the Shore board (photo 3).

4   Use the white colored pencil and mark a line all the way around the Shore board, about 1 inch (2.5 cm) in from the outer edge (photo 4).

5   Paint the space inside the pencil mark with the white house paint (photo 5).

6   Set the boards aside to dry.

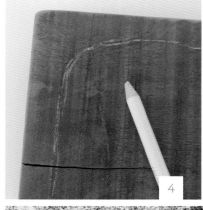

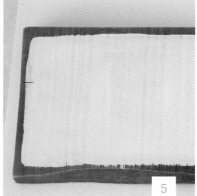

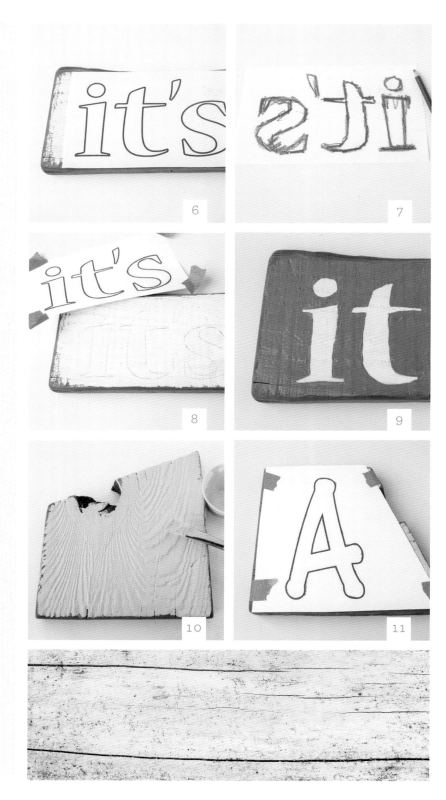

7   Trace all the words and letter templates onto copy paper.

8   Starting with the *it's* board, place the *it's* paper on top of the board and trim around the edges so you can see the board (photo 6). Flip the it's paper to the back side and trace over the letters with the side of the soft lead pencil (photo 7).

9   Flip the paper back to the front and tape in place. Trace over the letters with the regular pencil. Lift the paper and check to make sure that the letters transferred (photo 8).

10 With a small brush, outline the it's on the board with the blue paint. Fill in the board around the word with the blue paint (photo 9).

11 Paint the *A* board with the mint green paint (photo 10).

12 Follow steps 8 and 9 to transfer the *A* to the board (photo 11).

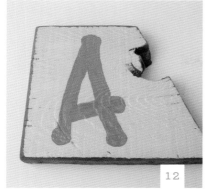

12

13

14

15

16

17

18

13 Using a small paintbrush, paint the letter A with teal paint (photo 12).

14 Using a thin paintbrush, add a thin boarder to the outer edge of the board with the light purple paint (photo 13).

15 Using the light aqua paint and a medium-size paintbrush, paint the *Shore* board on top of the white area, completely covering the white area (photo 14).

16 Follow steps 8 and 9 to transfer the word *Shore* onto the board.

17 Using a small paintbrush, paint the word *Shore* with teal paint.

18 Paint the *th* board with the light blue paint (photo 15).

19 Follow steps 8 and 9 to transfer the *th* to the board (photo 16).

20 Using a thin paintbrush, outline the *th* with the dark purple (photo 17).

21 Fill in the *th* with the light purple.

22 Paint a thin boarder around the *I* board with the mint green paint. Add a couple of stripes to the bottom of the board (photo 18).

23 Apply a coat of blue paint to the front, sides, top, and bottom of the *I* cutout (photo 19).

24 Paint the *ng* board with the mint green paint, stopping ½ inch (1.3 cm) from the outer edge of the white paint (photo 20).

25 Follow steps 8 and 9 to transfer the *ng* to the board (photo 21).

26 Using a small brush, outline the *ng* with the teal paint (photo 22). Fill in the board around the *ng* with the teal paint, leaving the white border exposed.

27 From the back, screw the *I* cutout onto the *I* background board, centered and 1 inch (2.5 cm) from the bottom.

28 Once all the paint is dry, lightly sand all the painted surfaces to give them that weathered, old sign look.

29 Flip the boards over onto a protected surface, wrong side up, and in the position that you want them arranged.

30 Place the three support boards onto the back of the sign and screw into place with the electric screwdriver (photo 23).

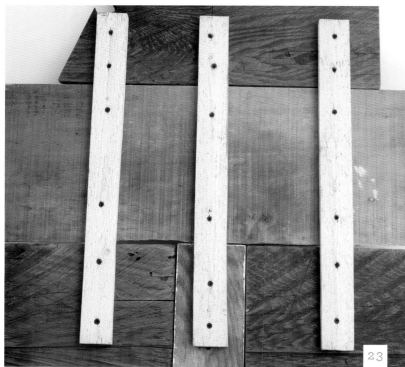

Knotted
COASTER SET

While you might be tempted to keep these coasters for yourself, they make the perfect gift for a nautical lover who not only entertains in the backyard but also hosts parties on the boat.

WHAT YOU NEED TO GATHER

White cotton cord, ³⁄₁₆ inch (.5 cm); (4 yards (3.6 m) are needed to make 1 coaster; 9 yards (8.2 m) are needed to make 1 trivet). To make a set of 4 coasters and 1 trivet you will need 25 yards (22.8 m).

Ruler

Acrylic paint: light blue, aqua, teal, and white

White glue

Water

Small disposable containers

Old paintbrush

¼ yard (23 cm) light blue craft felt

Pencil

Scissors

What You Do

COASTERS

1 Cut a length of cotton cord 4 yards (3.6 m).

2 Following the first photo, make a pretzel figure with the cord with one short end and one long end. The short end of the cord should be 12 inches (30.5 cm) long after this step (photo 1).

3 Extend the loops of the "pretzel" to be about 4½ inches (11 cm) long (photo 2).

4 Twist the bottom loop up and then twist the top loop up (photo 3).

5 Cross the top loop over the bottom loop and even out the cord shape (photo 4).

6 Pick up the short end of the cord and weave it through the cord shape, under the center scallop and then over the next two cords, then under the top right loop (photo 5).

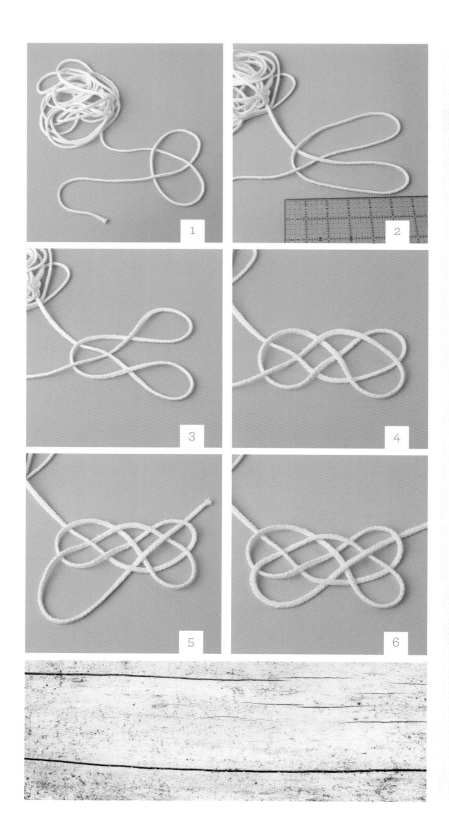

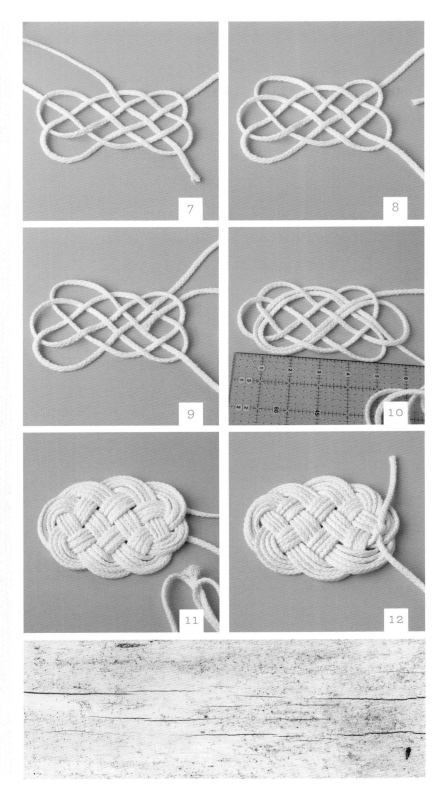

7 Pull the short cord to balance the knot (photo 6).

8 Pick up the end of the long cord and then weave it through the knot. Starting at the top center scallop, go over this cord, then under the next cord, over the next cord, under the next cord and then, finally, over the bottom right loop (photo 7).

9 Carefully pull all the cord from the long end through this sequence (photo 8).

10 Using the long cord, bring the end up to the point where the short cord exits the knot. This is the beginning of round 2 for the knot (photo 9). Follow the weaving pattern of the knot as established in the previous steps.

11 With every pass of the cord, stop and adjust the cords so that they start to stack up against each other (photo 10).

12 Continue weaving until four passes are complete (photo 11).

13 Knot the short end and the long end together on the back of the coaster and then cut the cord close to the knot (photo 12).

14 Mix together 1 tablespoon (15 mL) of light blue acrylic paint, 1 teaspoon (5 mL) of water, and 1 teaspoon (5 mL) of white glue in one of the disposable containers.

15 Brush the paint and glue mixture on the knotted coaster (photo 13). Flip the coaster over and paint the back and the sides. Place the coaster on a plastic surface and let it dry (photo 14).

16 Place the coaster on the felt and trace around the perimeter (photo 15).

17 Cut out the traced shape ¼ inch (6 mm) inside the pencil mark (photo 16).

18 Add glue to the back of the felt piece (photo 17) and then press it onto the knotted coaster (photo 18).

19 For the remaining three coasters, follow steps 1–18.

Note: *This set has coasters of four different shades. To create them, paint one coaster with light blue paint. Paint the second coaster with the same light blue paint, plus 1 teaspoon (5 mL) of white paint added. Paint the third coaster with aqua paint. Paint the fourth coaster with the same aqua paint, plus 1 teaspoon (5 mL) of white paint added.*

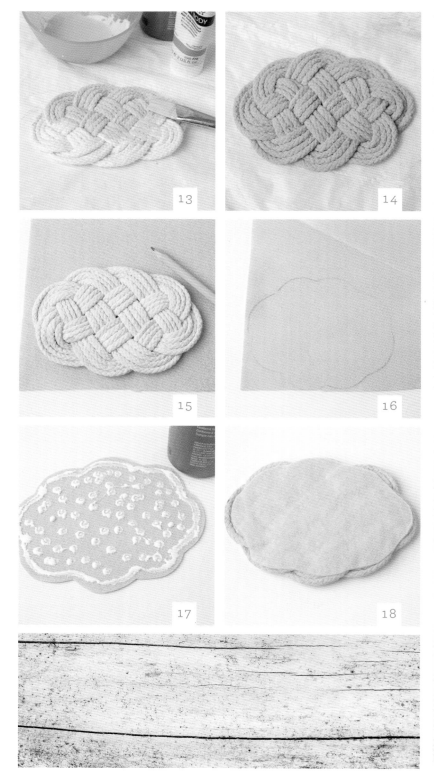

19

TRIVET

1 Cut a length of cord 9 yards (8.2 m).

2 Following the first photo, make a pretzel figure with one short end and one long end. The short end of the cord should be 20 inches (51 cm) long after this step.

3 Extend the loops of the "pretzel" to be about 6 inches (15 cm) long.

4 Twist the bottom loop up and then twist the top loop up.

5 Cross the top loop over the bottom loop and even out the cord shape.

6 Pick up the short end of the cord and weave it through the cord shape, under the center scallop and then over the next two cords, then under the top right loop.

7 Pull the short cord to balance the knot.

8 Pick up the end of the long cord and then weave it through the knot. Starting at the top center scallop, go over this cord, then under the next cord, over the next cord, under the next cord, and then, finally, over the bottom right loop.

9 Carefully pull all the cord from the long end through this sequence.

10 Using the long cord, bring the end up to the point where the short cord exits the knot. This is the beginning of round 2 for the knot. Follow the weaving pattern of the knot as established in the previous steps.

11 With every pass of the cord, stop and adjust the cords so that they start to stack up against each other.

12 Continue weaving until six passes are complete.

13 Knot the short end and the long end together on the back of the trivet and then cut the cord close to the knot.

14 Mix together 1 tablespoon (15 mL) of teal acrylic paint, 1 teaspoon (5 mL) of water, and 1 teaspoon (5 mL) of white glue.

15 Brush the paint and glue mixture on the knotted trivet. Flip the trivet over and paint the back and the sides. Place the trivet on a plastic surface and let it dry.

16 Place the trivet on the felt and trace around the perimeter.

17 Cut out the traced shape ¼ inch (.64 cm) inside the pencil mark.

18 Add glue to the back of the felt piece and then press it onto the knotted trivet.

Message in a bottle
NECKLACE

Make a fresh, elegant necklace by mixing metal chain with some thin cording, string, a few mother-of-pearl buttons, and some coconut shell beads.

WHAT YOU NEED TO GATHER

Thin rayon cord in gray (21 inches or 53 cm), dark brown (17 inches or 43 cm), and light green (31 inches or 79 cm)

3 ⅜-inch (1 m) dark brown coconut shell beads

4 ¼-inch (11.5 cm) light brown coconut shell beads

Ruler

1 2-inch (5 cm) pewter-colored head pin

1 green glass bead (⅝ inches or 16 mm) high and 1 inch (2.5 cm) in circumference)

Round-nose jewelry pliers

Chain-nose jewelry pliers

1 ⅜-inch (1 m) jump ring in antique brass

1 ¾-inch (2 cm) mother-of-pearl ring

2 ⅜ inch (6 cm) square mother-of-pearl buttons

2 ⅜ x ½ inch (2 x 1.3 cm) oval mother-of-pearl buttons

2 ¼ x ½ inch (2.2 x 1.3 cm) rectangular mother-of-pearl buttons

1 large shell bead, ¾ x 1⅜ inches (2 x 3.5 cm)

6 small shell beads

Tiny glass bottle with a cork (1¼ inches [3.2 cm] tall and 1¾ inches [4.5 cm] in circumference)

1 sheet of copy paper

½ teaspoon (2 mL) of sand

Small scrap of old book text

Kitchen scissors

Large-eye needle

White glue

Tan string, 6 inches (15 cm)

Small pearl

Jewelry glue

Tiny screw eye

4¼ inch (11 cm) jump ring in dark pewter

Chain, 34 inches (86 cm)

6 pewter-colored clam shell bead covers

Pewter-colored lobster clasp

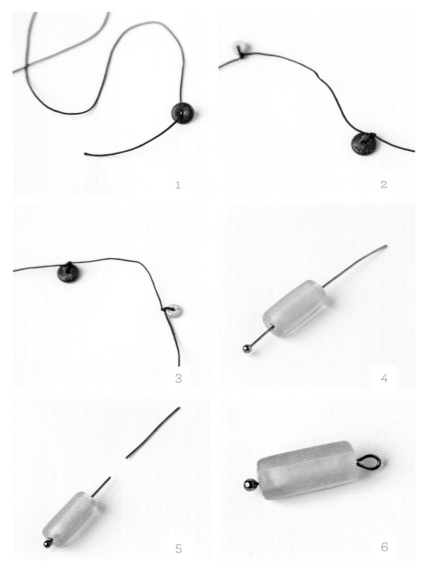

What You Do

1   Tie one of the dark brown coconut shell beads to the center of the dark brown cord (photo 1).

2   Tie two light brown coconut shell beads onto the dark brown cord on either side of the first bead, 3 inches (7.6 cm) apart (photos 2–3).

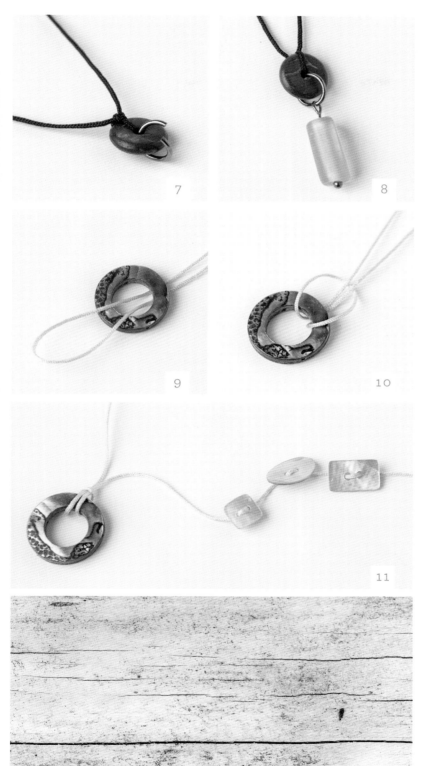

3 Tie two dark brown coconut shell beads onto the dark brown cord, 3 inches (7.6 cm) away from the last beads.

4 Tie the last two light brown coconut shell beads to the dark brown cord, 3 inches (7.6 cm) away from the last beads (photo 3).

5 Insert the head pin into the green glass bead (photo 4).

6 Cut the end off using the jewelry pliers, leaving ⅝ inch (2 cm) (photo 5).

7 Use round-nose pliers and create a loop at the end (photo 6).

8 Use chain-nose pliers and open the ⅜-inch (1.9 cm) jump ring. Hook the jump ring into the centered brown coconut bead and then into the pin head loop (photo 7). Place the green bead on the jump ring and close the jump ring (photo 8). Set the strand aside.

9 Fold the light green cord in half and insert it into the center of the mother-of-pearl ring to create a small loop (photo 9) and then loop the ends of the cord through that loop and pull snug (photo 10).

10 Thread the mother-of-pearl buttons onto the cord starting with the square button; next, the oval button; and, then, the rectangular button. Repeat for the opposite side. Space the buttons 2 inches (5 cm) from the mother-of-pearl ring and ¾ inch (2 cm) apart from each other (photo 11). Set the strand aside.

11 Fold the light gray cord in half and insert it into the center of the large shell bead to create a small loop (photo 12) and then loop the ends of the cord through that loop and pull snug (photo 13).

12 Create a single overhand knot in the gray cord on either side of the shell, 1 inch (2.5 cm) away (photo 14).

13 Thread a small shell bead onto the cord and then push up against the knot (photo 15). Create another knot close to the shell bead (photo 16).

Note: *To get the knot right up against the shell bead, while it is still open and loose, insert a pin in the middle near the bead and then tie the knot at the pin.*

14 Create another knot ½ inch (1.3 cm) from the last knot. Thread another small shell bead onto the cord and then knot it again, close to that bead. Repeat this step for the remaining small shells. Set this strand aside (photo 17).

15 Remove the cork from the glass bottle. Create a funnel shape with copy paper and insert the small end into the bottle. Pour the sand into the bottle (photo 18).

16 Tear a piece of old book text, measuring ⅝ x 1¼ inches (2 x 3.2 cm) (photo 19).

17 Roll the book text paper onto a large-eye needle (photo 20). Add a small amount of white glue to the paper at the beginning and then at the end (photo 21). Slip the needle out from the center (photo 22).

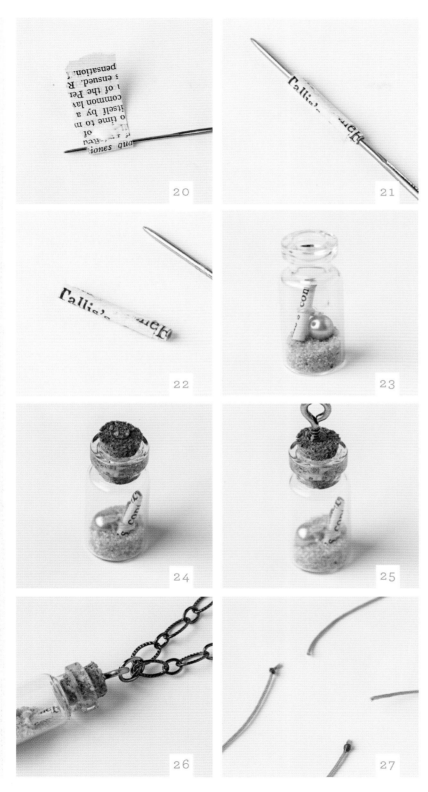

18 Tie the tan string around the book text roll and knot. Trim the ends of the string close to the knot. Slip this message into the bottle and then drop a pearl in (photo 23).

19 Apply a small amount of white glue to the cork and then push the cork into the top of the bottle (photo 24). Set aside to dry.

20 Place a drop of jewelry glue on the top of the cork at its center. Carefully screw the eye screw into the cork (photo 25). Set aside to dry.

21 Attach a ¼-inch (.64-cm) jump ring to the eye screw and then thread it onto the chain (photo 26).

22 Arrange all the necklace strands on a flat surface.

23 Knot the ends of the cords with a simple overhand knot. Apply a small amount of jewelry glue to the knots and set them aside to dry. Trim off any excess cord close to the knot (photo 27).

24 Close the knots inside the clam shell bead covers (photo 28).

25 Attach a ¼-inch (6 mm) jump ring to all the strands and then attach the jump ring to the lobster clasp. Repeat for the remaining side.

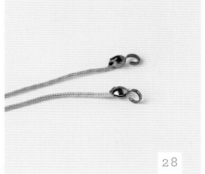

Nautical
FLAGS

WHAT YOU NEED TO GATHER

¾ yard (70 cm) off-white drill fabric

Pinking shears

Acrylic paint: white, red, black, blue, and yellow

Ruler

Pencil

Fine-tip black permanent marker

Sewing machine or white glue

Iron and pressing cloth

6 yards (5.5 m) off-white string

Kitchen scissors

Safety pin

Nautical flags, or signal flags, are used as a means of communication between boats at times when radio communication has been silenced. While each flag has a specific meaning, each also denotes a letter in the alphabet. For example, the flag for letter D represents delta, which signifies *I am maneuvering with difficulty. Keep clear.*

The flags can be strung together in alphabetical order or lined up to send out a variety of messages or to spell out a word or name. For this project, you will be painting these flags on fabric, and you can arrange and rearrange the flags to spell the family name or to add a special word or quote to a mantel or to decorate a child's room. You can even stencil one or more flags on a pillowcase with the initials of over-night guests to make them feel special and welcome.

What You Do

1   Cut out a 5 x 5½ inch rectangle from a piece of cardboard. Place the cardboard rectangle onto the drill fabric and trace 26 rectangles.

2   Cut out the rectangles using the pinking shears (photo 1).

3   Take the cardboard rectangle and cut out a 4 x 4 inch square from the middle. There will be a ½ inch border at the sides and a 1 inch border at the top and bottom. Place this cutout on top of a fabric rectangle and paint the center portion with white paint. Set aside to dry (photos 2–3).

4   Using a pencil and ruler, mark the nautical flag lines. Follow the chart on the opposite page.

5   Paint the red and blue portion of the flag and set aside to dry (photo 4).

6   Using a black permanent marker and the ruler, draw a line around the perimeter of the flag (photo 5).

7   Fold the top edge of the flag down ½ inch (1.3 cm) and machine stitch in place, creating a channel for the string to tunnel through. If you don't have a sewing machine an alternative is to add a line of glue to the top edge and then fold it down in place, making sure that the glue does not spill into the tunnel.

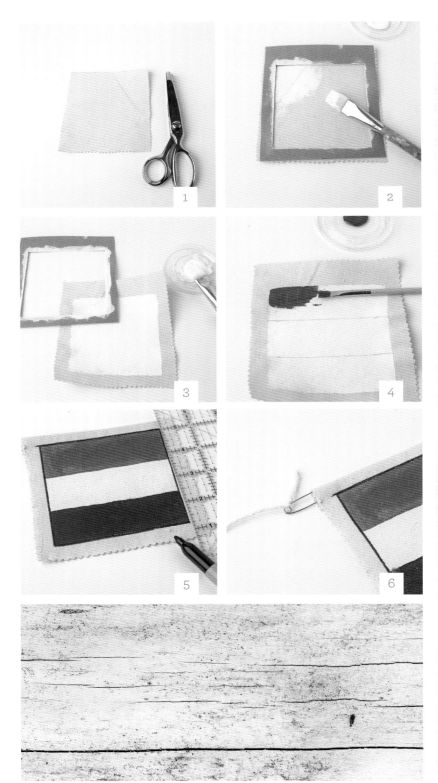

8   Repeat steps 3–7 for the remaining 25 nautical flags.

9   Place a pressing cloth on an ironing board and lightly press the flags flat.

10   Arrange the flags in alphabetical order. Cut the string into four strands of 50 inches (127 cm) each. Create a knot in the end of the strings.

11   Poke a safety pin into one of the knots and then tunnel the pin through the top channel in the flag (photo 6). Repeat for all the remaining flags.

Driftwood
SEASIDE VILLAGE

Transform a couple of pieces of driftwood into a bait house, lighthouse, and cottage—a few of the necessary elements needed for a seaside village.

WHAT YOU NEED TO GATHER

10 chunks of driftwood

Sandpaper

Pencil

Acrylic paint: Light blue, midnight blue, red, white, and yellow

Several small paintbrushes

Acrylic spray sealer

What You Do

1   Sand the bottom of a piece of driftwood to allow the piece to stand up.

2   Draw a house with a chimney on a chunk of wood with a pencil. Draw a second, smaller house on the wood, overlapping the first house at the roof (photo 1).

3   Paint the larger house and the chimney with light blue paint. Once the paint is dry, apply a second coat (photo 2).

4   Paint the smaller house and the roof of the larger house with red paint. Once the paint is dry, apply a second coat (photo 3).

5   Paint the roof on the smaller house and the front door on the larger house with midnight blue paint. Once the paint is dry, apply a second coat (photo 4).

6   Paint the front door of the smaller house with yellow paint, and the windows with white paint. Once the paint is dry, apply a second coat.

7   With the white paint, add little details to both houses. Paint the front doorknobs and paint polka dots on the eaves of the smaller house (photos 5–6).

8   Paint thin stripes with midnight blue paint on the roof of the larger house.

9   Outline the houses and their roofs, windows, chimneys, and front doors with the pencil.

10 Spray a thin coat of acrylic spray sealer on the painted houses.

11 Repeat for all the other driftwood pieces. Paint houses, lighthouses, bait shops, and birds (photo 7).

Sand
MEMORABILIA

Beach house vacations or lakeside campouts can be remembered with just a few sandy plaster essentials that can be displayed on a tabletop or in a child's bedroom.

WHAT YOU NEED TO GATHER

Plastic container, 15 x 10 x 5 inches (38 x 25.4 x 13 cm)

Play sand (enough to almost fill the above plastic container)

Water

Rubber spatula

Small plastic turtle, sunglasses, plastic rake, and wood numbers (2, 0, 1, and 5)

Disposable containers

Plaster of Paris, 8-pound (3.6 kg) container

1-cup (240 mL) measure

½-cup measure (120 mL)

Plastic fork and spoon

What You Do

1   Fill the plastic container with about 3 inches (7.5 cm) of play sand (photo 1).

2   Add water to the sand until it is completely wet and can hold some peaks (when you pinch the wet sand, the sand can stand up like a little peak). If you add too much water, just dump a little more sand into the mixture (photo 1).

3   Use a spatula to flatten out the sand in the container (photo 2).

4   Press the plastic turtle mold upside down into the flattened sand. Use your fingers to pack the sand into the sides of the mold, then carefully lift it up and off the sand, leaving an impression (photo 3).

5   In a disposable container, mix the plaster of Paris according to the manufacturer's instructions. Use a fork to mix the plaster, stirring until all the lumps are gone (photo 4).

6   Carefully spoon the plaster mixture into the turtle impression. You need to work quickly, as the plaster will start to harden within just a few minutes (photo 5).

7   Let the plaster completely dry before lifting the plaster turtle out of the sand. If you touch the turtle while it is drying, the plaster will at first feel warm, and then it will feel cool. Once it is hard and cool, you can take the turtle out of the sand (photo 6).

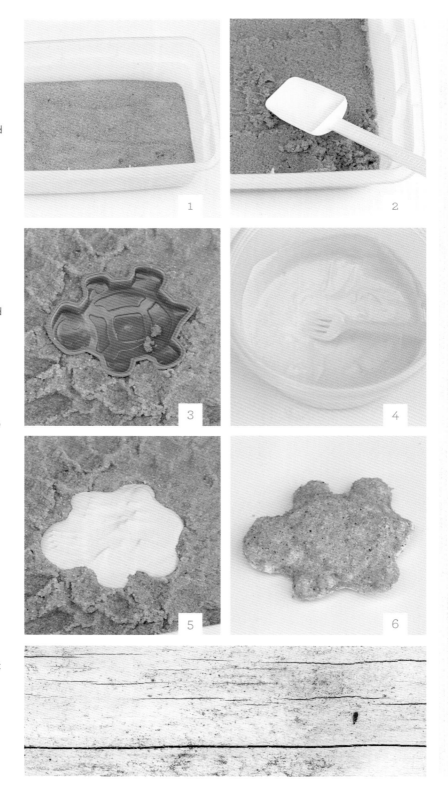

8 Allow the plaster to dry out completely overnight, and then, once completely dry, brush off the excess sand to reveal the details in the turtle (photo 7).

9 Throw the leftover plaster and the container in the trash. Do not rinse it out in the sink! The plaster will eventually harden and could completely block the drain.

10 Repeat steps 3–9 to create the other pieces of plaster memorabilia.

River rock
CLOCK

This simple and sophisticated clock is a fresh way to display the pebble and stone collection you've been gathering from all of your coastal travels and vacations.

Kitchen scissors

10-inch (25.4 cm) light-weight wood circle, 3 mm thick

Scrap paper, 12 x 12 inches (30.5 x 30.5 cm)

Pencil

White acrylic paint

Foam brush

Sandpaper

Drill with a $\frac{5}{16}$ inch (8 mm) drill bit

Epoxy

2 pieces driftwood, cut in half with a handsaw

Approximately 200 river rocks or pebbles, ranging in size from 1¼ inch (3.2 cm) to ½ inch (1.3 cm), in a variety of colors

Clock movement kit for ¾-inch (2-cm) thick surface and $\frac{5}{16}$-inch (8 mm) shaft

What You Do

1   Trace the wood circle on the scrap paper and cut out the circle (photo 1).

2   Fold the circle in half (photo 2), and fold in half again (photo 3).

3   Unfold the paper and place a mark at the center where the two folds meet, and at the outer edge of each fold (photo 4).

4   Paint the wood circle with the white paint and set aside to dry. Once dry, lightly sand the wood (photo 5).

5   Place the paper circle on top of the painted wood circle and mark the wood at the folds and at the center (photo 6). To mark the center, poke a small hole in the center of the paper with a pencil and then mark the center point of the wood. To mark the wood at the side folds, shift the paper up slightly to reveal the wood at the bottom, then shift it up to reveal the wood at the top, and then do the same for both sides (photo 6).

6   Drill a ⁵/₁₆-inch (.8 cm) hole in the center of the wood at the mark. Lightly sand the painted surface (photo 7).

7   Mix a small amount of the epoxy and then apply to the flat surface of the split driftwood pieces. Press the driftwood onto the wood circle at the four marks on the edges (photo 8).

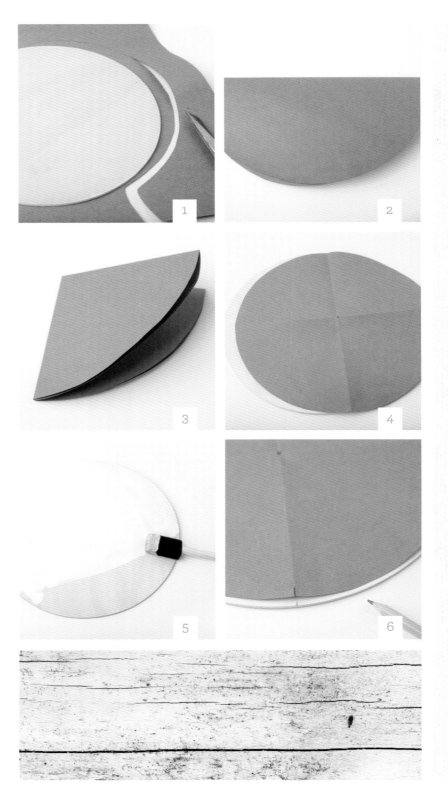

8 Mix up a small amount of epoxy and apply to the flat side of a rock, pressing into the wood circle. Use the remaining rocks or pebbles, and start adhering them around the outer edge, moving gradually toward the center (photo 9). The epoxy will dry fast so it's best to mix up small batches at a time. At the center, near the drilled hole, leave a space of about ¾ inch (2 cm) free from any rocks (photo 9). Set aside for 24 hours to let the epoxy fully cure.

9 Attach the clock movement pieces according to the directions on the package.

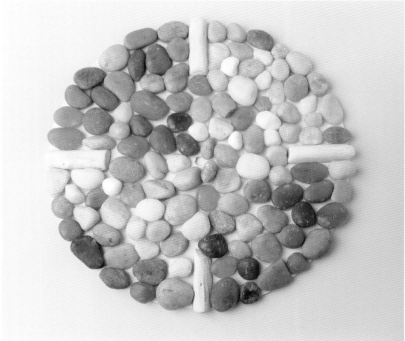

tip

If some of the epoxy gets on any of the rocks, gently sand it off with a tiny piece of sandpaper. Use epoxy to adhere the back portion of the clock movement unit to the back of the clock.

Sand
LETTERS

These easy-to-make sandy letters will welcome friends and family to any front porch and create a lazy summer seaside escape.

WHAT YOU NEED TO GATHER

Three-dimensional letters to spell a name, approximately 5 x 8 inches (13 x 20 cm)

White and red acrylic paint

White glue

Paintbrush

Old paintbrush

Sand

Sandpaper

Walnut ink

Soft cloth

What You Do

1   Paint the craft-colored letter white (photo 1).

2   Drizzle glue on the front of the letter (photo 2). Use a generous amount and then spread the glue out evenly across the front of the letter using an old paintbrush (photo 3).

3   Sprinkle a generous amount of sand over the glue-covered surface and then pat the sand down with your hand (photo 4). Lift the letter up and allow the excess sand to fall off (photo 5). Allow the glue to dry completely before moving on to the next step.

4   Squeeze out dots of glue on the letter, evenly spaced along one of the front straight edges (photo 6).

5   Sprinkle a generous amount of sand on the dots. Lightly tap the sand into the dot, but not so much that the dot is smashed flat. Lift the letter up and allow the excess sand to fall off. Allow the glue to dry completely before moving on to the next step (photo 7).

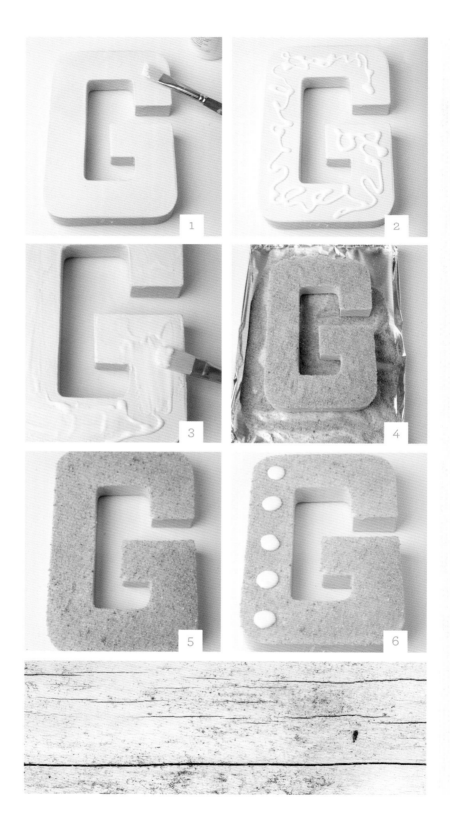

6   Paint the sides of the letter red. Once the paint has dried, lightly sand the sides of the letter so that the white paint and the craft-colored paper start to show through (photo 8).

7   Using a clean cloth, rub walnut ink on the sides of the letter and allow the ink to dry (photo 9).

8   Repeat steps 1–7 for the other letters.

Sand *and Jute*

CANDLESTICKS

With just a bit of sand, paint, and jute, transform mismatched candlesticks into fresh seaside candlesticks worthy of any coffee table or mantel.

3 wood or metal candlesticks in a variety of shapes and heights (short candlestick: 4½ x 7 inches [11 x 18 cm]; medium candlestick: 3½ x 7½ inches [8.9 x 19 cm]; tall candlestick, 5 x 9 inches [13 x 23 cm])

Sandpaper, 100 grit

Off-white spray paint

White glue

Paintbrush, stiff and old

Plastic spoon

Sand

Jute, 2 mm 3-ply, approximately 10 yards (9 m), depending on the size and shape of the candlesticks

Kitchen scissors

Tan burlap strip, 1 x 20 inches (2.5 x 51 cm)

4 starfish

What You Do

1 Lightly sand the surface of one candlestick.

2 Spray paint the candlestick with the off-white paint. Note: This does not need to be a perfect, even coat of paint; the off-white paint allows the sand to stay light in color. Lightly sand the candlestick again.

3 Cover the work surface.

4 Using the old paintbrush, apply a generous coat of glue to a small portion of the candlestick (photo 1).

5 Scoop up a spoonful of sand and pour it over the surface of the candlestick where the glue was applied (photo 2).

6 Lightly pat the sand into the glue. Tap the edge of the candlestick on the work surface to loosen any excess sand (photo 3).

7 Apply glue to another portion of the candlestick and again spoon sand over the glued surface (photo 4).

8 Continue to apply glue and sand until the entire surface of the candlestick is covered in sand. Remember to add sand to the top surface of the candlestick where the pillar candle will rest (photo 5).

9 Set the candlestick aside and allow the glue to dry completely.

10 Once the glue has dried, gently tap the candlestick on the work surface to release any excess sand.

11 Look closely at the candlestick and decide where the jute will be wrapped. (Look for divets or dips in the candlestick where the jute can be wrapped.)

12 Apply glue straight from the bottle around the candlestick where the jute will be wrapped. Smooth the glue with the paintbrush (photo 6).

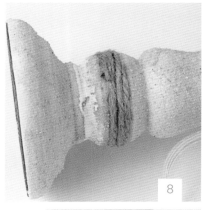

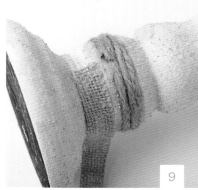

13 Cut off a generous length of jute and begin wrapping around the candlestick. Overlap the beginning point of the jute with the next wrap-around (photo 7).

14 Continue wrapping the jute around the candlestick, adding glue to areas where needed as you go. Stop wrapping the candlestick with the jute when the wrapped area is about 1 inch (20.5 cm) high (photo 8).

Note: *Every candlestick is different so you may want to make the jute-wrapped areas wider or narrower.*

15 Apply glue to the candlestick just under the jute-wrapped area, and wrap a thin strip of burlap around the glued surface (photo 9). Trim off the excess burlap.

16 Apply glue to the upper portion of the candlestick and wrap a second thin strip of burlap around the glued surface. Trim off any excess burlap.

17 Cut a length of jute and tie it around the candlestick over the above burlap strip (photo 10).

18 Lay the candlestick on its side. Add a dot of glue to the back of the starfish and press into the jute. Hold the starfish in place for a few minutes to ensure it is adhering to the jute (photo 11).

19 Repeat steps 1–18 for the two remaining candlesticks.

Sand and Jute Candlesticks   109

Heart
WREATH

Make this one-of-a-kind shell–encrusted wreath to adorn any mantel, glass cabinet, or mirror—or simply lay it flat to double as a centerpiece for a table or dresser.

WHAT YOU NEED TO GATHER

Kitchen scissors

¼ yard (23 cm) polyester batting

Tape measure

12-inch (30.5 cm) wire heart wreath frame

Hot glue and hot glue gun

½ yard (46 cm) white muslin

½ yard (46 cm) off-white burlap

White acrylic paint

Paintbrush

300 seashells ranging in size from 3 inches to ½ inch (7.6 x 1.3 cm)

1 large starfish, 2¾ inches (7 cm), and 2 smaller starfish, 1¾ inches (4.5 cm)

White linen scrap, 2 x 8 inches (5 x 20 cm)

Dremel tool and small drill bit

White thread

Hand needle

What You Do

1   Cut the batting into three segments measuring 5 x 20 inches (13 x 51 cm).

2   Wrap the batting around the wire heart lengthwise and secure with hot glue (photos 1–2).

3   Tear the muslin into four strips of 2½ x 45 inches (6.4 x 114 cm) (photo 3).

4   Wrap the muslin around the batting, securing the ends with hot glue (photo 4).

5   Cut the burlap into four strips of 2½ x 45 inches (60 x 114 cm).

6   Wrap the burlap around the muslin, securing the ends with hot glue (photo 5).

6

7

7 Paint the seashells white (photo 6).

8 Hot glue the shells to the heart. Start by placing the largest shells around the heart. Fill in the gaps with the smaller shells. Glue some of the shells on the wreath upside down to add interest (photo 7).

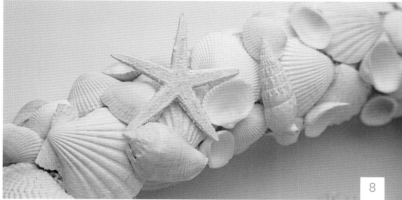

8

9 Glue the two smaller starfish to the wreath, one at the bottom right and one at the top left (photo 8).

10 Tie the small linen strip in a knot and hand sew it to the inside of the wreath (photo 9).

11 Drill a small hole through the large starfish.

12 Stitch through the drilled hole and sew the large starfish to the knotted linen strip (photo 10).

9

10

Starfish

GREETING CARDS

Simple stencils transform a few sheets of card stock and old book text into one-of-a-kind all-occasion greeting cards. Pair these cards with a couple of handmade pencils for a delightful birthday or hostess gift.

WHAT YOU NEED TO GATHER

Starfish, 2¼ x 2¼ inches (5.7 x 5.7 cm)

2 sheets white card stock

Pencil

Kitchen scissors

Craft knife

2 foam stencil brushes

Navy blue ink pad

White paint marker

1 page of book text

Double-sided tape

3 craft-colored cards, 5 x 7 inches (13 x 18 cm)

White ink pad

1½ yards (137 cm) white cotton string

Scotch tape

3 white envelopes, 5¼ x 7¼ inches (13 x 18 cm)

What You Do

1   Trace the starfish onto a piece of card stock (photo 1) and cut out around the shape to create the stencil (photo 2).

2   Place the stencil on the other sheet of white card stock and, using a foam stencil brush and navy blue ink pad, fill in the starfish shape (photo 3).

3   Cut out around the starfish you just created (photo 4).

4   Add dots of white paint using the paint marker (photo 5).

5   Repeat steps 2–4 six more times to make a total of seven blue starfish.

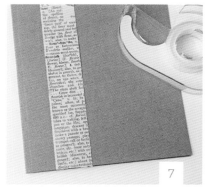

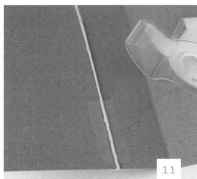

VERTICAL STARFISH

1 Cut a strip of book text 1 x 7 inches (2.5 x 18 cm) and adhere it with the double-sided tape to a craft card, ⅞ inch (2.2 cm) away from the folded edge (photo 7).

2 Using a foam stencil brush and white ink, fill in the strip of card that is between the book text strip and the folded edge (photo 8).

3 Cut a strip of white card stock ¼ x 7 inches (.64 x 18 cm) and adhere it with the double-sided tape, centered over the book text (photo 9).

4 Arrange three stenciled starfish on the card and adhere with the double-sided tape (photo 10).

5 Cut a length of cotton string 19 inches (48 cm) and tie it around the card, centered over the book text strip. Secure the string to the card by placing two strips of Scotch tape to the inside flap (photos 11–12).

6 Add little white dots to the card with the white paint marker (photo 10).

7 Stencil a starfish to the back flap of the envelope. Add dots of white to that starfish (photo 13).

STARFISH

1. Cut a strip of book text 1½ x 7 (3.8 x 18 cm) inches and adhere it to a craft card, ¾ inch (2 cm) away from the right edge (photo 14).

2. Using a foam stencil brush and white ink, fill in the strip of card to the right of the book text (photo 15).

3. Cut a strip of white card stock ¼ x 7 inches (.64 x 18 cm) and adhere it, centered over the book text (photo 16).

4. Arrange one stenciled starfish on the card and adhere (photo 17).

5. Cut a length of cotton string 19 inches (48 cm) and tie it around the card, centered over the book text strip (photo 18). Secure the string to the card by placing two strips of Scotch tape to the inside flap (photo 19).

6. Add little white dots to the card (photo 20).

7. Stencil a starfish to the back flap of the envelope (photo 21). Add dots of white to that starfish.

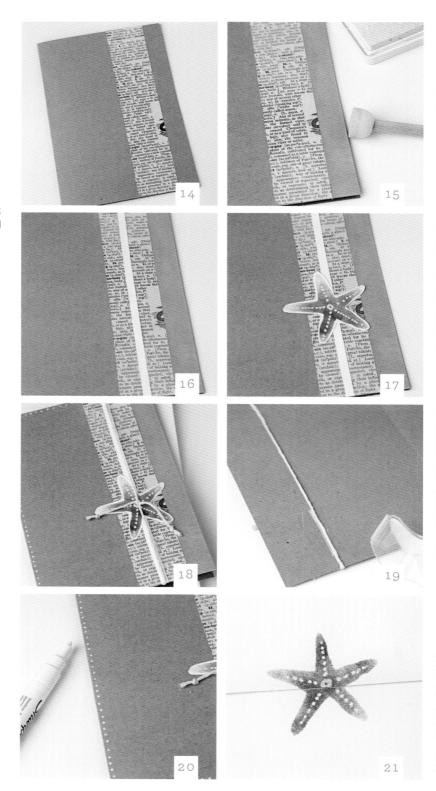

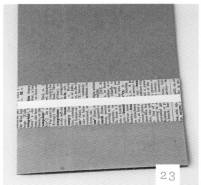

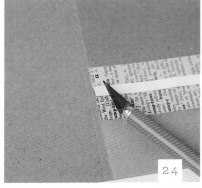

22

23

1. Cut a strip of book text 5 x 1½ inches (13 x 3.8 cm) and adhere it to a craft card, 1½ (3.8 cm) inches up from the bottom edge (photo 14).

2. Using a foam stencil brush and white ink, fill in the strip of card that is under the book text (photo 22).

3. Cut a strip of white card stock ¼ x 5 inches (.64 x 13 cm) and adhere it, centered over the book text (photo 23).

24

25

4. Cut a length of cotton string 14 inches (36 cm). Open the card up and slit the fold ¼ inch (.64 cm) where the narrow white strip is. Tie the string around the card, threading it into the slit and then around the card (photo 24). Secure the string to the card by placing two strips of Scotch tape to the inside flap.

5. Arrange three stenciled starfish on the card and adhere (photo 25).

6. Add little white dots to the card (photo 26).

26

7. Stencil a starfish to the back flap of an envelope. Add dots of white to that starfish (photo 21).

Linen seashell
PILLOWS

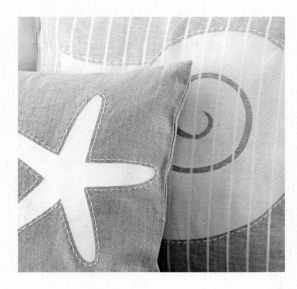

These easy, low-sew, stenciled pillows add that perfect touch of seaside elegance to any cottage or guest bedroom.

WHAT YOU NEED TO GATHER

1½ (1.6 m) yards of natural colored linen

⅝ yard (57 cm) of natural and white striped linen

Kitchen scissors

Tape measure

3 yards (2.7 m) freezer paper, 18 inches (46 cm) wide

Pencil

White copy paper

Craft knife

Iron and ironing board

White matte spray paint

Hand sewing needle

White perle cotton thread or embroidery floss

Sewing machine

Tan thread

Pins

Pillow forms: 16 x 12 inches, 18 x 18 inches, and 16 x 16 inches (30 x 41 cm, 46 x 46 cm, 41 x 41 cm)

Pillow Template A (page 141)

Pillow Template B (page 141)

Pillow Template C (page 141)

What You Do

TWO-STARFISH PILLOW

1 From the solid colored linen, cut one panel 17 x 13 inches (43 x 33 cm) for the front of the pillow, and two panels 10½ x 13 inches (27 x 33 cm) for the back of the pillow.

2 Cut one panel of freezer paper 17 x 13 inches (43 x 33 cm).

3 Trace Pillow Template A onto copy paper and cut it out.

4 Trace the starfish cutout onto the paper side of the freezer paper panel twice, evenly spaced (photo 1).

5 Use the craft knife to cut out the traced starfish shapes (photo 2).

6 Iron the freezer paper, shiny side down, onto the large linen panel (photo 3).

7 Place the linen panel on a protected surface and spray paint the linen with the freezer paper over it. Spray several even coats, allowing the paint to dry between each coat (photo 4).

8 Once the paint has completely dried, peel the freezer paper off the linen (photo 5).

9 Hand stitch a long running stitch around the perimeter of the starfish with the white perle cotton (photo 6).

10 Press ½ inch (1.3 cm) under one of the long sides of a back panel to form a hem (photo 7). Using a sewing machine, stitch the hem in place (photo 8). Repeat for the other back panel.

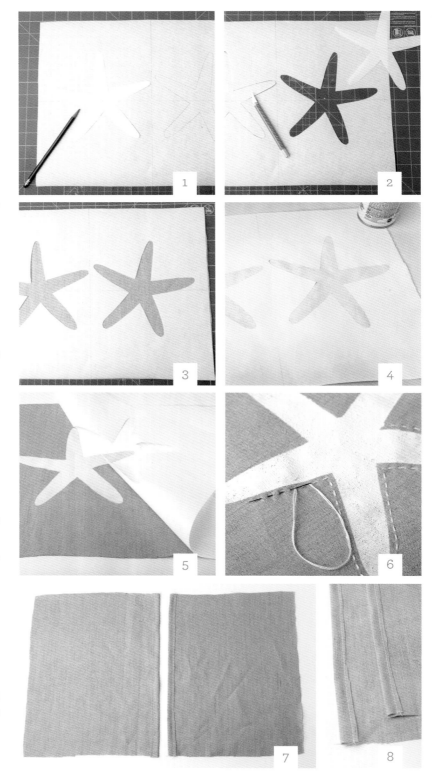

9

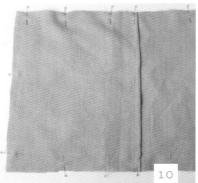

10

11

12

11 Place one of the back panels onto the front panel, right sides facing, aligning the top, right side, and bottom edges, and pin in place (photo 9). Place the second back panel on top of the front panel, aligning the top, left side, and the bottom edges and pin in place (photo 10). The two back panels will overlap at the center portion.

12 Machine stitch around the perimeter of the pillow with ½-inch (1.3 cm) seam allowance.

13 Trim the fabric diagonally at each corner and then turn the pillow right side out (photo 11).

14 Stuff the pillow with the 16 x 12–inch (30 x 41 cm) pillow form (photo 12).

SAND DOLLAR PILLOW

1   From the solid-colored linen, cut one panel 19 x 19 inches (48 x 48 cm) for the front of the pillow, and cut two panels 11½ x 19 inches 29 x 48) for the back of the pillow.

2   Cut one panel of freezer paper 19 x 18 inches (48 x 46 cm).

3   Trace Pillow Template B onto copy paper and cut it out.

4   Center the sand dollar cutout on the paper side of the freezer paper panel and trace around the shape.

5   Use the craft knife to cut out the traced sand dollar shape.

6   Iron the freezer paper, shiny side down, onto the large linen panel.

7   Place the linen panel on a protected surface and spray paint the linen. Spray several even coats, allowing the paint to dry between each coat.

8   Once the paint has completely dried, peel the freezer paper off the linen (photo 13).

9   Hand stitch a long running stitch around the perimeter of the sand dollar with the white perle cotton.

10 Press ½ inch (1.3 cm) under one of the long sides of a back panel to form a hem. Using a sewing machine, stitch the hem in place. Repeat for the other back panel.

11 Place one of the back panels onto the front panel, right sides facing, and pin in place. Place the second back panel on top of the front panel and pin in place. The two back panels will overlap.

13

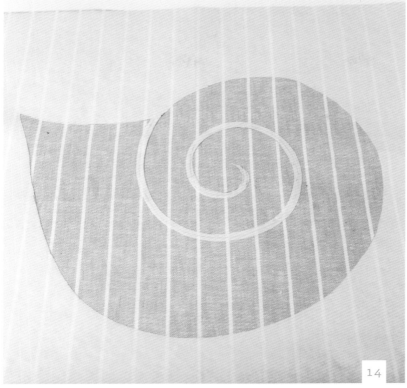

14

12 Machine stitch around the perimeter of the pillow with ½-inch (1.3-cm) seam allowance.

13 Trim the fabric diagonally at the corner and then turn the pillow right side out.

14 Stuff the pillow with the 18 x 18 inch (46 x 46 cm) pillow form.

SHELL PILLOW

1 From the striped linen fabric, cut one panel 17 x 17 inches (43 x 43 cm) for the front of the pillow, and cut two panels 10½ x 17 inches (27 x 43 cm) for the back of the pillow.

2 Cut one panel of freezer paper 17 x 17 inches (43 x 43 cm).

3 Trace Template C onto copy paper and cut it out.

4 Center the shell cutout on the paper side of the freezer paper panel and trace around the shape.

5 Use the craft knife to cut out the traced shell shape.

6 Iron the freezer paper, shiny side down, onto the large linen panel.

7 Place the linen panel on a protected surface and spray paint the linen. Spray several even coats, allowing the paint to dry between each coat.

8 Once the paint has completely dried, peel the freezer paper off the linen (photo 14).

9 Hand stitch a long running stitch around the perimeter of the shell with the white perle cotton.

10 Press ½ inch (1.3 cm) under one of the long sides of a back panel to form a hem. Using a sewing machine, stitch the hem in place. Repeat for the other back panel.

11 Place one of the back panels onto the front panel, right sides facing, and pin in place. Place the second back panel on top of the front panel and pin in place. The two back panels will overlap.

12 Machine stitch around the perimeter of the pillow with ½-inch (1.3-cm) seam allowance.

13 Trim the fabric diagonally at the corner and then turn the pillow right side out.

14 Stuff the pillow with the 16 x 16- inch (41 x 41-cm) pillow form.

8

Stick PENCILS

Handmade pencils make the perfect accompaniment to stationery or greeting cards.

WHAT YOU NEED TO GATHER

1 dry stick, at least 12 inches (30.5 cm) in length and 2 inches (5 cm) in diameter

Sandpaper, 100 grit

Handsaw

Ruler or tape measure

Black marker

Drill with ³⁄₃₂ drill bit

2 lengths of 2-mm lead

5-inch (13-cm) pipe cleaner

White glue

White acrylic paint

Small container for paint

Water

Small paintbrush

Soft cloth

Pocketknife

What You Do

1 Sand the stick to smooth the outer surface (photo 1).

2 Saw the stick into two 6-inch (15 cm) lengths (photo 2).

3 Mark the center of the cut surface and drill into the stick as far as your drill bit will allow (photo 3).

4 Slip the lead into the drilled hole to make sure it fits. Take the lead out of the hole.

5 Dip the pipe cleaner in white glue and insert it into the drilled hole, moving it in and out (photo 4). Dip the pipe cleaner back in the white glue and insert it again, spinning it around.

6 Slip the lead into the hole and set it aside to dry (photo 5).

7 Put a small amount of paint in a container and add a few drops of water. Stir the mixture and then paint the stick (photo 6). Wipe off excess paint.

8 Use a pocketknife and whittle the end of the stick into a point (photo 7).

9 Repeat steps 3–8 for the second stick.

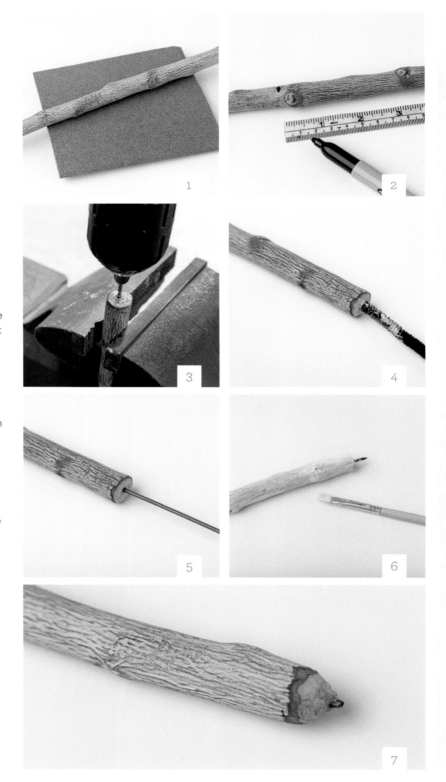

Stitched
FISH GARLAND

Stitch up your fresh catch of the day and hang it from a mantel or dresser—or perhaps in a fish tank, tabletop, or as centerpiece for your next fish fry feast.

WHAT YOU NEED TO GATHER

Kitchen scissors

Fish Template A (page 142)

1 yard (1 m) muslin to make 12 fish

White thread

Hand sewing needle

1 bag of Fiberfill

Pencil or chopstick

Straight pins

Acrylic paint: white, mint green, light blue, and gray

Paintbrush

Large-eye needle

5 yards (4.5 m) thin jute rope

What You Do

1   Copy the Fish Template A and trace it onto two layers of muslin (photo 1), then cut out the fish (photo 2).

2   Hand sew the fish using an overcast stitch (photo 3). Start sewing at the edge of the fish and end on the same side, leaving a 2-inch (5 cm) gap unstitched (photo 4). Do not knot or cut the thread.

3   Stuff the fish with Fiberfill, using a pencil or chopstick to help push it into the tail end and the head (photo 5).

4   Pin the opening closed and continue stitching and then knot the thread (photo 6).

5   Paint the fish with a generous amount of white paint and then set the fish aside to dry (photo 7).

6   Repeat steps 1–5 for the remaining 11 fish.

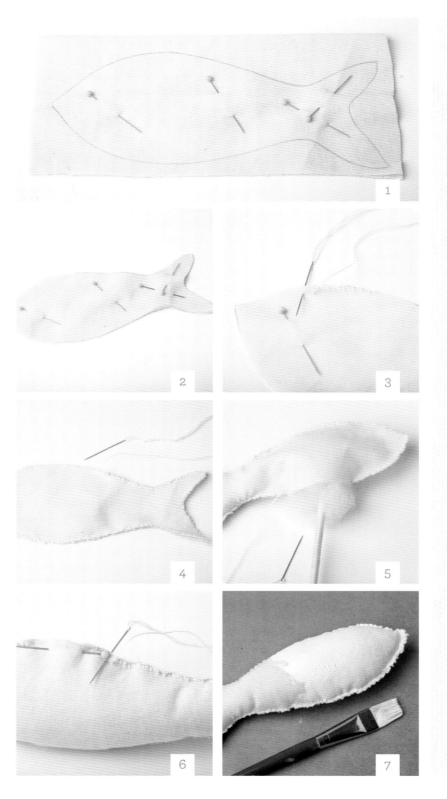

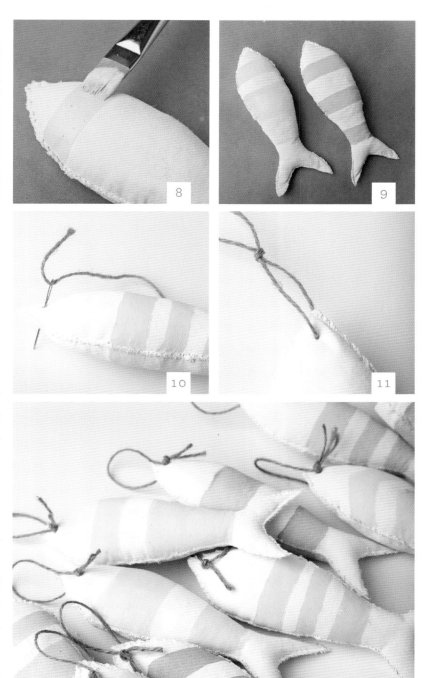

7   Paint green, blue, or gray stripes on the fish, varying the widths and spacing of the stripes to add interest (photo 8). Paint some of the fish with chevron stripes (photo 9).

8   Cut the jute rope into nine 7-inch (18-cm) lengths. Thread a length of jute through the large-eye needle. Stitch through the nose of a fish (photo 10) and then knot the jute (photo 11), shifting the knot toward the fish. Repeat for the other 11 fishes (photo 12).

9   String up all the fish onto the remaining jute rope.

Templates

Anchor and Sailboat

Garland and Gift Toppers

Sailboat Embroidered Dish Towels

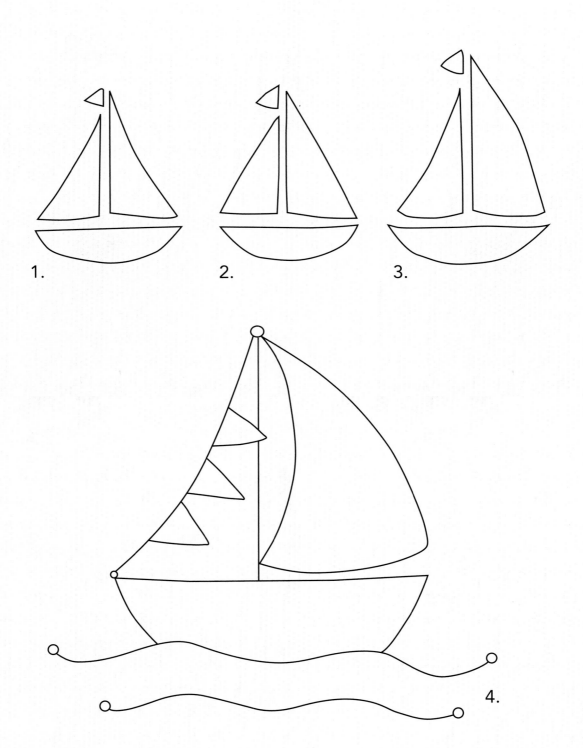

1.

2.

3.

4.

Coral Vases

A

B

C

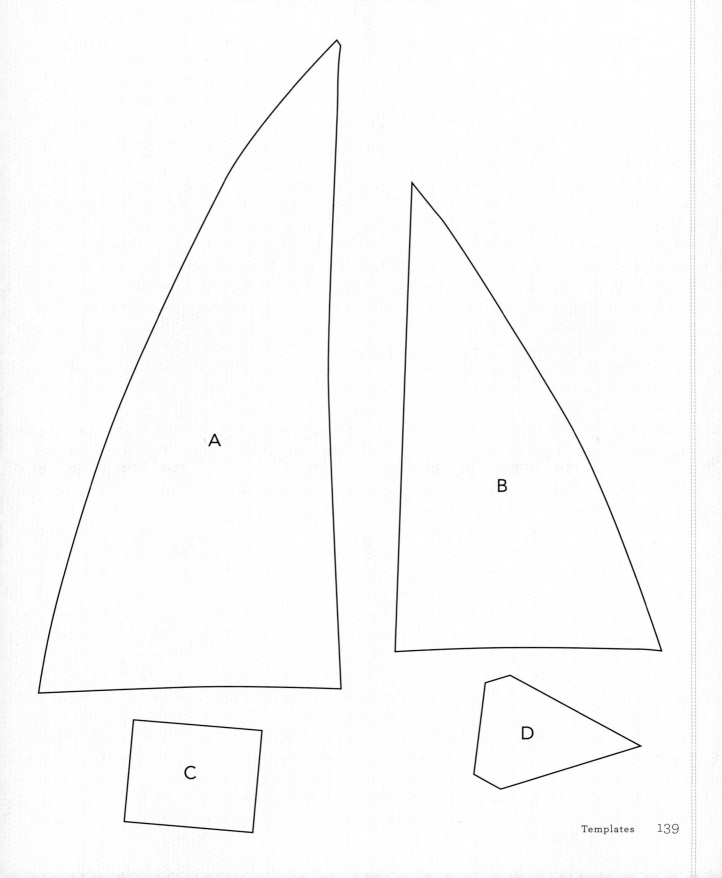

A

B

C

D

Templates

It's A Shore Thing Wall Hanging

it's A
Shore
thing